The Little Dark Spot:

How I Came to Terms with My Baby's Stroke

The Little Dark Spot:

How I Came to Terms with My Baby's Stroke

Helene Louise

MICHABOOKS

Acknowledgements

I would like to acknowledge Geneviève S. for her invaluable support in editing and structuring this story, Katherine M. for her gentle encouragement throughout the process and Hélène H. for helping me find the courage to get started at all.

A Note to the Reader

This book reflects the individual experience of the author. Neither the author nor the publisher is engaged in rendering medical or any other type of professional advice or services to the reader. The ideas, reflections and examples contained in this book are not intended as a substitute for consulting with a physician or other qualified health practitioner, nor are they intended as an example of what may be possible or appropriate for others. All matters regarding your health and that of your children require medical supervision. Neither the publisher nor the author shall be liable or responsible for any loss, injury or damages, including, but not limited to, physical, emotional, psychological and financial, arising from anything contained in this book.

For information contact:
Micha Books at info@michabooks.ca

ISBN 978-0-9918048-0-1
Printed and bound in Canada.
www.michabooks.ca

To all the children whose tiny triumphs are cause for celebration and the adults whose hard work makes it all possible

Table of Contents

Preface

All social change comes from the passion of individuals.
Margaret Mead

In writing this book, I can't claim to be setting out to achieve the kind of social change that Margaret Mead was probably referring to in this quote. However, in many ways her words resonate with my experience coming to terms with my daughter having suffered a stroke and my motivation for sharing our story. Receiving that terrible diagnosis and at the same time, being given a tremendously discouraging opinion as to what her future would look like, was one of a series of setbacks that marked the beginning of a very difficult period in my life—it was a time of great emotional pain, or *passion*, in the sense of "suffering" as it is sometimes defined.

One of the things that I think prolonged my suffering, is the emotional isolation I felt at that time. Had I been able to find a meaningful reference point to draw on, something to help me organize my thoughts and, most importantly, give me a sense of perspective and hope, I think that I could have come to terms with what I was facing much sooner than I did. Had that been the case, I think that I would also have been able to help my daughter even more than I have. But even now, many years later, there are very few materials available for parents in similar situations.

Perhaps that is simply because raising children is already challenging enough and when a child has a serious condition, there isn't much time left over to reflect on the experience, let alone document it so that it can be shared with others. In my case, however, writing about my experience has brought me a sense of healing and resolution. And, it is the very fact that I eventually found strength and beauty through such a difficult time that left me with a *passion* in the other sense of the word—in the sense of a "strong drive and feeling of conviction to do something". If this book brings just a glimmer of hope and perspective to one person's life, then I will consider that my *passion*, in both the sense of "suffering" and "conviction to do something", will have succeeded in bringing about a small change for the better.

Nevertheless, it is important to note that this story represents the individual *passion* of only one person—me. It is my version of a series of events and interactions as I experienced them. I recognize that the perspectives of those who were around me at the time may be different from what I have written here. Even so, what I have to offer is an honest account of how I felt when I found out that my baby had suffered a stroke, how my feelings about events and relationships at that time shaped my decisions, how I approached my daughter's rehabilitation, and eventually, how I came to terms with it all, realizing that even the most difficult situations can, with time, bring something positive.

If I could somehow reverse my daughter's stroke, I would do it in a heartbeat. But I can't and to my own relief, despite the emotional suffering of the past, there is much to be thankful for in the present. I greatly appreciate the support of the many professionals who have facilitated my daughter's rehabilitation such that her future is as bright as anyone else's. I am very thankful for all of my dear friends who helped me work through my emotional pain once

I managed to start talking about it and ultimately, have so generously supported me in my *passion* to transform my experience into something positive, beyond my own daughter's progress. I am thankful for my family and most of all, I am truly thankful for my daughters, from whom I have learned so much about love, compassion, forgiveness and understanding.

—Helene Louise

Introduction

My daughter Amelia (Mimi) was born on a beautiful fall day. She was the most adorable baby that I had seen since her sister Charlotte was born almost three years earlier. From the hospital window I could see the sun shining brightly through the brilliantly coloured trees. I was elated. I had two beautiful daughters, both in good health. I was married, I had a wonderful group of friends and I had a house with a small garden that I loved working in. I had much to be thankful for. In a way, Mimi's arrival signalled the realization of my lifelong dream. What I truly wanted most of all, was a happy and fulfilling family life. Somehow, with two children, my life seemed complete. We weren't just a couple. We weren't just a couple with a child. We were a couple with two daughters. We were a family.

From the day she was born, Mimi was a good-natured baby and overall, she seemed to be developing much in the same way as her older sister had at the same age. The only difference was that it seemed that Mimi might be left-handed. Because her father is left-handed, I didn't think much of it. But, as the months went by, I started to wonder if it wasn't that Mimi was favouring her left hand as much as it was that she was *only* using her left hand. With their spindly, uncoordinated limbs that flail around indiscriminately, and their tiny hands that they haven't yet learned to use, it's hard to gauge whether a baby is moving "normally" or not. Besides, there is so much else to focus on—the challenges of making sure that they are thriving, the relentless feeding and diapering routine and of course, the distracting happiness that comes from holding them close. But still, somewhere inside of me an uncomfortable concern began taking root.

A few months later, rather than starting to crawl, Mimi preferred to sit on the floor and push herself along sideways. We called it "scooching" and joked that Mimi was doing a great job of buffing the floors with her diaper. But, silently and steadily, the creeping roots of that uncomfortable concern continued to grow until finally, when Mimi was about eight months old, I asked my family doctor what she thought. After many tests, Mimi was diagnosed as having suffered a stroke—a "cerebrovascular accident". They called her condition "left hemiplegia". The specialist who gave me the news held up a blurry image and told me that it was a picture of Mimi's brain. He pointed to a little dark spot on the image and said that what it meant, was that at some point, a random clot had travelled to the end of an artery somewhere in my baby's brain and caused the damage which was that little dark spot.

I heard the words coming out of his mouth but they didn't make sense as they entered into my head. Why was he talking about something that happens to old people when I was there to talk about my baby? As far as I was concerned, strokes only happen to people of a "certain age", people who already have many vibrant years behind them and who, in those years, may have willingly lived with increased risk factors. Mimi didn't fit into that category. I had certainly spent the pregnancy doing everything that I possibly could to stay healthy, including exercising and maintaining a healthy diet. Mimi herself had, of course, never smoked or had a poor diet. She had barely begun eating solid foods at all. Yet, there it was—a stroke was the specialist's explanation for Mimi's "scooching" and strong preference for her left hand. He went on to say that, as a result, Mimi would likely never walk and even if she ever did, it would be with a significant limp. Finally, he added that she would probably be developmentally delayed.

Through the waves of nausea that were now sweeping over me, I asked him desperately what I could do to help her. There was nothing to be done, he said, the stroke was permanent. But I couldn't accept that answer so I continued to press him for options. The only advice he had to offer was that I should just "learn to live with it." The finality of his words and the fact that they communicated a complete lack of hope was unbearable. But I couldn't help it, I had to ask again if there wasn't anything, anything at all, that I could do to at least *try* to help my baby. His response, more as an aside than anything else, was that if I really wanted to, I could try physiotherapy although in his opinion, it "wouldn't be worth the trouble".

Never in my life have I felt so overwhelmed and broken as I did at that moment. I couldn't even begin to accept that there was nothing I could do to help my beautiful baby, even a little. I asked myself how the blurry picture of Mimi's brain that he had just shown me could possibly mean, with all certainty, that my only option was to "learn to live with" the consequences of that little dark spot. This situation did not fit into my usual outlook of hopefulness even against the odds, and hard work even in the face of uncertainty.

As I tucked Mimi into her car seat to go home, she smiled happily at me. In my mind, I was frantically processing what I had just heard. But in my heart, I simply couldn't reconcile the label and limitations that the specialist had placed on her with the intelligence and perceptiveness I saw in her bright eyes. I didn't know what impact this would have on our lives and I had no idea what I was going to do about it. But, I knew with absolute certainty, that I couldn't accept the label and limitations as is and just "learn to live with it" as I had been told to do. Well, I might have to accept the label, because a stroke is a stroke after all. I had seen the picture that was now tucked away somewhere in Mimi's file and I had seen the spot that showed where the damage had been done by that wayward clot. But I didn't have to accept, and I simply could not accept, the limitations that had been placed on her, at least not without a good fight.

What followed was an intensely difficult period in my life as I struggled to learn more about what could be done for my daughter and what I could do to encourage her to achieve her full potential, whatever that might mean for her. It wasn't easy to gain access to the occupational and physiotherapists who could provide me with the guidance I needed. And, since I could find no relevant materials to inspire or motivate me, it felt as if I were searching for something in the dark without knowing exactly what it was that I was trying to find. After all, what was I aiming for when the specialist had told me that it wouldn't be worth the trouble to do anything?

I was desperate for a ray of hope, anything, however faint to which I could anchor my thoughts and actions in order to find my way. Through the many sleepless nights and anxiety-filled days that followed, the conversation with the specialist replayed over and over again in my mind. Gradually, I realized that ironically, the only semblance of a ray of hope lay within the specialist's own words. There was nothing positive about what he had said, of course, and he had been far from hopeful. Nevertheless, somewhere in the conversation that was looping in my mind, I started to focus on what might possibly be interpreted as an *element of doubt*. The specialist had said that Mimi would likely never walk. Maybe, "likely never" didn't necessarily mean "absolutely for certain she will never walk". He had said that she would probably be developmentally delayed. Maybe, "probably" didn't necessarily mean "absolutely for certain she will be developmentally delayed". Admittedly, it was weak as far as rays of hope go but in the absence of anything else, it was all that I had to go on and it would have to do.

So, not long after that appointment, I started working hard to help Mimi learn to walk despite what the specialist had told me. I came up with different ways to help her learn to keep her balance although it was clearly much more difficult for her to do so. I held her tiny hands in mine and smiled at her encouragingly. At the same time, I held in my fear and pain, and when I simply couldn't hold the tears back any longer, I would turn around, let the most rebellious ones escape, wipe them away, turn back around and keep on smiling at my happy baby. Mimi didn't know that there was a problem and, as much as I could, I was not going to contaminate her childhood with something as heavy as this. If it turned out one day that the specialist was right about everything, I would worry about that then. In the meantime, Mimi was a happy baby and I was going to keep it that way.

To my great amazement, with a lot of patience and perseverance, and a lot of tears wiped away so that no one could see, Mimi made progress. She was wobbly and she did limp but she could balance herself and put one foot in front of the other to get wherever she wanted to go. She could walk–absolutely and with all certainty. In the absence of a reference point for what was possible, this development magnified my faint ray of hope into a *reason to persevere*. It reinforced my commitment to helping my daughter as much as I could. Maybe, even if I hadn't tried to help her in the way that I did, she would have learned to walk just the same. But the fact that the specialist had said that she likely never would and then she had learned anyway, set me on a path to believe in her and always question those who said that she wouldn't be able to do something.

As a result, I worked hard to get the advice that I needed to understand her situation and figure out how I might help her. Whenever I was told that something wasn't possible for her to do, I asked, "What if it *were* possible, what could I do then?" I pushed against all kinds of negativity and I never gave up on my commitment to help her achieve whatever her own potential might be. Each step of the way, Mimi continued to surprise everyone with her brilliant determination, endless creativity and tremendous capacity to overcome the limitations placed on her. As almost imperceptible as each step towards improvement was, each one was a tiny triumph and each one was something to be appreciated and celebrated.

Now, ten years later, Mimi is a vibrant young girl who is doing fine in school, enjoys sports, plays the violin and is fully fluent in both English and French. She has exceeded all expectations. She knows how to work hard, she knows what it is to overcome challenges, she is confident and she has a strong sense of self. Most of all, she does not define herself in terms of the effects of that little dark spot. Some of those effects are still there and we're still working on them but compared to where we started, we have come a long way from that devastating appointment with the specialist.

As it turns out, despite the emotional pain and difficulties of the past ten years, there has been much to be thankful for. Along with the heartbreak, there has been hope, inspiration and success. Within the struggles and triumphs, no matter how ever-so-tiny those triumphs may appear to others, there has been beauty and grace. Had I known what was possible with patience and perseverance and how much hope there actually was, this journey would have been much less difficult. Had I had the benefit of someone sharing their experience with me—a story in which I could recognize my own feelings—this journey would have been much less isolating. It is with this in mind that I have written this book.

Initially, my objective was only to document how I dealt with my daughter's stroke in terms of the things I think I have done well and the things that I might have done differently, had I known then what I know now. However, as I started writing, I realized that I could not separate the way in which I dealt with this experience from everything else I had to cope with over that same period of time. The other major challenges, including the unravelling of my marriage, influenced the choices that were available to me. Under different circumstances, with different options, I may have done things differently. Because of that, what I am offering here is a much more personal account than I ever intended to share.

This is the story of how I came to terms with my daughter's stroke in the context in which I dealt with it. I hope that by honestly describing my experience, parents in similar situations may find their own feelings validated such that they can focus more clearly on the future and on achieving the best possible outcome for their child, whatever that means for them. And, even for those who are not facing a similar situation, in sharing the tiny and not-so-tiny triumphs that were ours to celebrate, perhaps they too will be inspired to persevere and focus on what is possible, rather than what is not.

1

Something's Not Quite Right

No matter what the circumstances are, it is a terrible feeling when you start to think that something's not quite right but you're not sure what the problem might be. In the case of my daughter, it started when I realized that it wasn't just that I thought she might be left-handed, it was that I wasn't actually sure if I ever saw her using her right hand at all. I casually asked my friends and family if they thought there might be something to worry about but no one seemed particularly concerned.

I remember very vividly, however, the moment when my slight concern spontaneously transformed into a sickening feeling in the pit of my stomach. I was holding Mimi in my arms and I took her right hand into mine. I ran my thumb upwards along the base of her fist expecting her hand to open at some point but it didn't. I ran my thumb all around her closed-up hand again and again but no matter what I did, her fingers stayed curled up in a tight fist. That can't be right, I thought. I started trying to open her fingers and finally, it took all the strength that I had in both of my hands combined, to pry open her hand and get her tiny fingers extended even slightly.

When I finally looked inside her fist, I was horrified by what I saw. Her entire palm was covered in a bright red rash, full of boils of all sizes. It was terribly damp in there and it smelled awful. I immediately felt an intense wave of guilt as I wondered how, in all of the times that I had so lovingly and carefully bathed her, I could possibly have missed something like that. I washed her hand right away and, as hard as it was to keep her fingers pried open, I kept them extended until I was certain that her palm was dry.

From that day on, many times a day, I would open up her right hand even though it was closed-up so tightly that my own hands ached from the exertion required to uncurl and extend her fingers. Each time, I made sure to clean the inside of her hand and expose it to the air so that it could dry out. In retrospect, although I had no idea at the time, the fact that I was opening up her hand and stretching out her fingers turned out to be critical to her ability to make progress and gain use of that hand as she got older. Slowly, the rash began to clear up although the sickening feeling in my stomach remained. Now I really felt something wasn't quite right but I wasn't sure how to formulate a question around that feeling. I couldn't very well go online and put "baby's stinky palm" or "closed-up infant hand" to an Internet search.

A few months later, when Mimi was about eight months old, she had a routine check-up. The doctor said everything was fine but throughout the appointment I was wondering whether or not I should ask about Mimi's hand and her "scooching". It wasn't until the appointment was over and I was already standing in the doorway, ready to leave, that I finally brought myself to say anything. In response to my question, however incoherent it may have been, the doctor took a tongue depressor and held it in front of Mimi who grabbed at it with her left hand. The doctor then put it near Mimi's right hand. Mimi moved her right hand in the general direction of the tongue depressor but did not grab onto it. The doctor said that she didn't know if there was anything to be concerned about but if I wanted to, she could refer me to a specialist.

I stood there in the doorway for what felt like an eternity. I had already been so uncomfortable as to how I might formulate a question to my own family doctor when all I had to go on was that something didn't seem quite right. My heart was pounding and all I wanted to do was leave but I heard myself saying that yes, I wanted a referral. I have sometimes wondered what would have happened if I hadn't said yes at that moment. The diagnosis would have ended up being the same but I would have missed the valuable early years in which I got started on Mimi's rehabilitation. This was one of the many times that I would listen to my intuition and realize long afterwards how important it had been that I had done so.

Eventually, of course, I had the devastating appointment with the specialist who finally gave me the reason for what I had been noticing. Unfortunately, that was not the end of our medical appointments, it was more like the beginning. Yes, the little dark spot on the picture showed that Mimi had suffered a stroke but now we needed to find out what might have caused it. Depending on whatever the underlying medical problem might be, the stroke in question was potentially only the first of what could be many more. More strokes meant more little dark spots along with the brain damage that those spots represented.

Throughout all of this, I continuously felt a deep sense of sadness as I wondered what kind of life my little Mimi was going to have. This certainly was not what I had pictured when I had daydreamed about having a family. Along with all of these thoughts there was a feeling of intense guilt, as I wondered why I was even allowing myself to think this way. After all, lots of people live through much worse. A feeling of hopelessness also washed over me at regular intervals as I questioned whether or not I could handle this on top of everything else that I already had to worry about. Under any circumstances, it's not easy to adapt to life with a new baby and at the same time, balance pre-existing responsibilities. Most people are already juggling family, work and financial concerns, and often, the needs of an older child who, with the arrival of a new sibling, is now competing for attention. At times, I felt completely overwhelmed—I was certain that I was already at the absolute limit of what I was capable of handling, both physically and emotionally. And yet, here was another major problem added to my list of responsibilities.

In my case, there was also an acute sense of fear. I was repeatedly asked, "Have you ever felt angry with your baby? Have you ever been so angry that you felt like you wanted to hurt your baby? Have you ever shaken your baby or left her with someone who might have hurt her? Have you ever dropped her, maybe?" The first person to ask me these questions was my family doctor. By that time, the early test results were beginning to show that the problem was related to some kind of brain damage although it was not yet clear what the problem was. I felt blind-sided by her questions. The person that I trusted the most with my health and that of my children, the person to whom I turned when we needed help, was now the person who was suddenly looking at me in a way that I had never seen before.

I was frightened by the expression on her face and I couldn't believe what I was hearing. It had never occurred to me that I might be accused of having caused whatever unknown problem there was. I looked at my doctor, speechless, but the way that she was looking back at me made it very clear that she was serious. She really believed that I might have done something to my daughter and she was waiting for an answer. I felt my face flushing with anger and shock. At the same time, I immediately felt intensely worried because

I thought she might interpret my discomfort as an indication that I might have done something to my baby, even though I knew that it couldn't be further from the truth. From the day she was born, Mimi had rarely been out of my sight. I loved my daughters more than anything else and I had most certainly never done anything at all that might have threatened their well-being, in any way.

That was the first of many occasions on which I would be treated with great suspicion. Again and again, I felt humiliated as different people, in different settings, looked at me doubtfully and asked me probing questions to see if I might spontaneously confess to some horrible act that would explain Mimi's condition. Meanwhile, all I was trying to do was to find out what the problem was so that I could help her. I was extremely fearful that I might be accused of having harmed her and of what the consequences of such accusations might be. Could they take her away from me? If they did, how could I prove that I hadn't done anything except love her and take care of her as well as I could?

Ultimately, one of the later tests showed that the brain damage that Mimi had suffered was deep inside her brain and could therefore not have been caused by anything external—like me mistreating her when I might have "felt angry". The doctors agreed that the damage had to have been caused by a clot that had travelled to the end of an artery, which meant that I was no longer under suspicion. Still, that particular test result came long after I had first taken the initiative to ask my doctor if there was anything to be worried about.

Adding more fuel to this unfortunate fire, was the fact that in the first few years following Mimi's diagnosis, as often happens when families find themselves facing difficult situations, my family life was starting to deteriorate. The hairline cracks that had long existed in my marriage and which I now realize I had been continuously glossing over to keep the overall picture bright and shiny, were deepening and becoming wider. To be clear, this situation was not at all a result of what we were facing with Mimi's diagnosis. It was more that these new challenges made the issues that were already fracturing the relationship more apparent. As the reality of dealing with Mimi's diagnosis intensified, the cracks steadily deepened until no amount of gloss application could fill the ever-widening gaps.

- ◆ -

It had started well, I thought. We met when I was in my first year of university and he was in his last. We became best friends. I felt that no one understood me like he did. There was nothing that we couldn't talk about and there was no one else with whom I would rather spend my time. After he graduated, it became a long-distance relationship—better a two-hour conversation with him on the phone and sporadic visits, than any amount of time spent, in-person, with anyone else. It seems strange now but at the time it had made sense. I had had a privileged childhood, but emotionally, it had been isolating. In that context, our long-distance relationship gave me the sense of belonging that I needed. In that relationship I felt accepted and loved. Still, I was chronically lonely. We had so many plans for the wonderful things that we would do together one day but there was always a "very good reason" why we never did any of them—distance, academic aspirations, professional responsibilities, family obligations, bad timing.

The years went by and eventually we found ourselves in the same city. We got married and I was convinced that now, finally, life would be good. Now, the happy times would begin in earnest. I had married my best friend. I had married the man that I had loved for so many years, the man that I wanted to spend my time with and with whom I wanted to have a family. The time of chronic loneliness was surely over, I thought. I was certain that as we started living our life together we would do all of those things we had always talked about—some uneventful, like cooking and running, and others more elaborate, like skiing and travelling. We would be there for each other, no matter what happened, no matter what we had to face.

Looking back, the conditions that would eventually make the reality of dealing with Mimi's stroke much more difficult were there from the very beginning. Although distance was no longer a factor once we were married, it seemed that no matter what we planned, there was often a "very good reason" that got in the way. It was a bad time at work so it was best not to take a vacation. There was a new and important project at work that required lots of overtime. There was a great new opportunity coming up so it was important to spend evenings and weekends preparing for it. There was just one more e-mail to send or just one more phone call to make which inevitably took longer than expected. If I said that I was disappointed, I was being "unreasonable" and "unsupportive".

As a result, the feeling of chronic loneliness that I had felt before we were married, never went away. And, although I didn't admit it to myself, the loneliness steadily evolved to the unsettling feeling that because I was never among the "very important reasons" of any given day, I didn't actually matter all that much. I tried hard not to let myself think about it. Having spent years waiting to be together, it seemed impossible that it wouldn't be working out. It must be me. Maybe my expectations were too high. Maybe I was too insecure. Maybe I was too demanding and maybe I really was "unreasonable". Either way, it was probably best not to talk about it with anyone and just try my best to fix it. Maybe I just needed to try harder. That's what I kept telling myself.

Financially, the marriage brought unexpected challenges

as well. As it turned out, we had very different spending habits. I had always been very responsible with my money but now, even with two salaries, I had far less than ever before. It didn't matter, I loved him, I was committed to the marriage and I would adapt. To deal with the financial situation, I set up a second bank account and on the days we were paid, I transferred an amount that would be kept separate from the rest. Later, that was the money we used for a down payment on a house.

After a couple of years I became pregnant. I was nervous but happy. I was certain that a baby would bring back the closeness I had felt before were married—the feeling of caring and friendship that had been so important to me. After all, having a family was one of the things we had talked about for years. It was something we both wanted. I couldn't wait to go to the first ultrasound appointment together and get a glimpse of our baby. With all of the "very important things" that always seemed to get in the way, I asked him to please, please be on time that day because the appointment was so very important to me. "Yes, yes," he said. But as the appointment drew nearer, I stood outside my office building, waiting alone, in the rain, with the inevitable sinking feeling that I so often had. He was late again—something about a "very good reason."

We almost missed the appointment but finally, made it to the hospital. I was indescribably happy to see our unborn baby but my heart was heavy with disappointment. I felt like an after-thought, like an inconvenient obligation to be slotted in among the more important activities of that day. I had assumed that even if I didn't matter enough to make it onto the daily priority list, then at least any child of ours most certainly would. How could they not? Any other scenario seemed unthinkable. This assumption, another hairline crack in the relationship, was a mistake that would later be reinforced many times over as I faced the challenges associated with Mimi's stroke.

At the first appointment with my family doctor, the one at which I finally managed to formulate a question around my feeling that something wasn't quite right, I was alone. He hadn't been available that day. It was the same thing for the appointment with the specialist who told me about the stroke and then said that all I could do was learn to live with Mimi's bleak future. Over the period of three years or so during which Mimi had a series of heart-breaking appointments at many different hospitals, I was always alone. There was always a "very good reason" that prevented my husband from coming with us, no matter when the appointment was, no matter what it was about.

It was the same for the physiotherapy, occupational therapy, speech and whatever other therapy appointments that followed. I was alone in the waiting rooms and in the treatment rooms. I was alone in trying to encourage Mimi to do whatever it was that she was supposed to do to help her progress and in comforting her as she cried through all of the tests and treatments. I didn't know that after a child reaches their absolute most hysterical cries, they move on to horrific growling sounds full of deep anguish. I was alone in hearing those too. They still haunt me.

As I looked around at the other parents in the waiting rooms where Mimi and I sat for hours at a time, I felt so isolated. I wished that there was someone there with me, someone to ask me how I was doing under these very difficult circumstances or pass me a tissue when, despite my best efforts, the burning tears defiantly leaked out anyway. Even after the appointments, my husband was too busy to talk to me about what had happened at the hospital that day, or listen to what the doctors and specialists had said. There were always so many "very good reasons".

On some level, I knew that I was not wrong in expecting that a husband and father should take an interest in the well-being of his family. I certainly needed to feel that he was interested in the girls and me and I absolutely needed his support. But I was used to keeping myself numb as to how painful it is to feel as if you are being ignored and that you don't matter. In that context, the fact that my husband said anything at all in response to me speaking to him seemed somehow generous. When it came to my children, however, it hurt even more. I could maybe accept that I didn't matter but the idea that our children didn't matter as much as the "very good reasons" of the day was too much to bear. I knew with all of my heart that they deserved to feel loved and supported. They deserved to know and feel that they truly mattered, no matter what. The problem was, that by the time I started realizing that the apparent lack of interest in my well-being extended to that of my daughters, I was also just beginning to uncover the reality of what I was facing with Mimi.

Besides the deep emotional pain of finding out that my baby had a very serious problem, there was an enormous time-pressure associated with the diagnosis. I was told early on that if Mimi was to make any progress at all, then all of the effort had to be made in the first two years of her life. After that, it would be too late. (Now I know that this is not entirely true but that is what I was told and that is what I believed.) However, the dilemma was that by that time, Mimi was already more than a year old and the waiting list at the nearest treatment centre was two years. This meant that by the time Mimi would finally have access to any help, she would already be three years old and it would be too late to make any significant progress.

The clock was ticking and half of the time in which I could help her was already gone. It was clear that my priority had to be getting Mimi whatever help I could before it was too late, with or without the support of my husband. The other problems, marital or otherwise, would have to wait. In the short-term, I had to figure out how to help my baby, and fast...

2

Trusting My Intuition—We're 98% Chimp

When I was a young girl, I loved reading the Nancy Drew mysteries. Growing up in the suburbs during the 1980s, there was a tremendous emphasis on conformity. In order to be "liked" and "accepted" you had to look a certain way, speak a certain way and you definitely had to dress a certain way, right down to the smallest details. At one point, not only did you have to have exactly the right kind of shoes (boat shoes with the right kind of sole for sailing although few of us actually ever set foot on a boat), the laces also had to be tied in just the right way. It wasn't written down anywhere, if you were lucky, somebody showed you and you in turn, showed the next kid. It was a stifling environment but it was all we knew. What I liked about Nancy Drew, was that even though she lived in an environment that was so clearly conservative and retro, she seemed to thrive. Despite the strict conformity, she was fiercely free-thinking, independent, accomplished, fearless and capable. Like many young girls, I found her inspiring.

In my teens, I started to focus more on non-fiction books and I particularly liked reading autobiographies. Again, in the suburban cocoon in which we lived, before cell phones, the Internet, unlimited long-distance calling and endless television programming available around the clock, losing myself in someone else's story became a window into life beyond the 'burbs. One story that particularly fascinated me was that of Jane Goodall and the time she spent with the chimpanzees in the Gombe forests. She looked like such a normal girl—young, beautiful, innocent and naïve—but the life that she was living was at the opposite end of the spectrum from where I was. The very reality of her existence seemed so impossible to me. In my environment, the underlying values were conformity and obedience. We were told what to learn and how to learn it and that's what we were expected to do. If a parent, teacher, or a guy in a lab coat told you something was a fact, then it was so.

There was essentially one way of doing things, there was one frame of reference that we were to adopt and reflect, and if you dared to deviate from that, for the most part, you were considered insolent. Where we weren't told by authority figures what we should think and do, our peers stepped in to make the parameters abundantly clear. There was not much room for interpretation or reinterpretation. There was not much room for flexibility or trying something outside of the expected norm. And yet, at the very same time, somewhere deep in the forests of Africa, was Jane, living in a tent, not only free from the social imperatives that surrounded the rest of us but in fact, doing quite the opposite. Instead of conforming and figuring out what she was "supposed to do" within the established social structure, Jane was quietly observing the unfamiliar and complex social structure of one particular group of chimpanzees.

One of the elements of Jane's story which I found especially compelling was that from the outset, she had done things entirely her own way. She had a profound love of animals and she knew that she wanted to spend her life working with them.

However, rather than pursue an education that would enable her to work in a related field, she travelled to Africa and began working as a secretary. One day, she called the renowned paleontologist, Louis Leakey, with the objective of making an appointment to talk to him about animals. He ended up hiring her, first as his secretary and later as a researcher.

From the very beginning, Jane followed her intuition. She did not accept the long-standing beliefs related to animals and their behaviour. Instead, she took her inspiration from her first teacher, her dog Rusty. From Rusty, Jane had learned that animals have personalities, minds and feelings. When it came to the chimpanzees, because they share 98% of our DNA and brain structure, Jane figured that they must also share many of our feelings. So, while the academic standard was to number the animals being studied to remove any potential emotional attachment, Jane gave them names. It was with tremendous fascination that I read about David Greybeard, a grey-chinned male, who was the first chimpanzee that Jane observed using a stalk of grass as a tool to "fish" for termites in a termite hill. This early observation alone changed the way that the world perceived chimpanzees as it was previously thought that only humans have the capacity to develop and use tools. I delighted in reading about Flo and her children, and I was touched by Gigi, who although she was unable to have babies of her own, was a loving "aunt" to many young chimps.

Jane's work proved that animals do in fact have feelings. We now know that beyond the genetic similarities between us and the chimpanzees, we also share a capacity for emotions like joy, sorrow and anger. We share behaviours like tickling and hugging. We also share a tendency towards close bonds between family members and others in the community. The bottom line was that in the same way Nancy Drew acted on a hunch, Jane had had the courage and conviction to follow her intuition, and in doing so, she successfully challenged the long-standing academic beliefs of the time.

Unlike Jane, I do not have a dog named Rusty as a teacher, but I do have a cat from whom I have learned a lot. Just after I was married, I found two tiny kittens in a banana box that had been left in a flowerbed one rainy evening. Because the kittens were obviously abandoned, I brought them home. They were so small that each one fit in the palm of my hand. Eventually, I found someone to take one of them but I couldn't bring myself to part with the other, a little tabby that I named Allie. Growing up, apart from a couple of budgies, I hadn't had any pets so I didn't know anything about taking care of a cat. Nevertheless, I started by feeding her and giving her water. Slowly, Allie showed me when she was happy, when she wanted to be left alone, when she wanted affection and when she was mad at me (there's no mistaking a stinky "greeting card" left in the middle of the floor after a longer absence...).

As Allie got bigger, I wanted her to learn to come to me when I called her. I wasn't sure how to go about it but I figured that if I took something that I knew she liked to sniff, like a smelly piece of cheese, and rewarded her with it every time I called her, then maybe she might learn. I started by saying her name when she was close by, eventually moving further and further away from her, still holding the smelly cheese. The more I did this, the more it seemed that Allie understood that when I called "Alllliiieee", it was worth her while to come to wherever I was.

At the beginning, Allie seemed to know her name better when I was holding an extra old piece of cheddar say, rather than a piece of mozzarella, not to mention how fast she came when I was holding a little piece of tuna! So, it is possible that instead of thinking "Allie" meant, "That's my name and I need to run to that lady whenever I hear it," Allie thought it meant, "Run fast to that lady because there is something seriously stinky to be sniffed!" Regardless, without the use of words to explain what I meant and with no knowledge of cats and their behaviour, I managed to figure out how to interact with my furry non-verbal friend and motivate her to do something that she otherwise might not have done. With time, it appeared to me that Allie understood that when she heard me say "Allie", it was some kind of reference to her little cat self. Even now, more than sixteen years later, Allie still comes when I call her (unless she is curled up somewhere in a particularly cozy spot).

I am not comparing a child who has suffered a stroke with a chimpanzee or with my cat Allie. However, what I have learned on this journey is how critical it is to develop, trust and, most importantly, follow your intuition. Despite that I was in a completely devastated and vulnerable state when the specialist told me it "wouldn't be worth the trouble" to do anything for my daughter, somewhere within myself my intuition was asking, *How can he be so sure about that? Who is he to judge what is worth the trouble to me or not?* Then again, he was, after all, a guy in a lab coat, in a position of authority within a highly regarded profession and I, only a mother in crisis in the middle of a crumbling marriage. Who was I to defy someone like him and question the validity of his professional opinion, drawn from years of specialized study?

Then again, who was Jane, a former secretary with no formal scientific education, sitting in a tent jotting down the comings and goings of the local chimps, to question and defy an entire academic system and established philosophy? Armed only with her pencil and notebook, a sense of purpose, persistence and a love of animals, Jane had proven that her intuition had been right all along. She successfully challenged longstanding conventions, deciphered a previously unknown world and revolutionized the way we think about animals. My goals as a mother were far less ambitious than those of my childhood hero Jane. But, similarly armed with a sense of purpose, persistence and a profound love for my daughters, I was prepared to follow my intuition in order to achieve the best possible outcomes for them.

Would Nancy Drew have stopped sleuthing just because someone told her it "wouldn't be worth the trouble"? I don't think so. Had Jane given up just because the "specialists" had said that all evidence pointed to her being wrong? No, certainly not. So, I would choose to follow in the footsteps of my childhood role models, listen to my intuition and push the boundaries as far as I could.

– ◆ –

The first time I followed my nascent maternal intuition was actually just before Charlotte was born. I was eight months pregnant and my blood pressure started to be dangerously high. During an ultrasound appointment to make sure my precious unborn baby was still doing fine, it was discovered that she was breech. Despite my doctor's attempt to turn her over so that she would be facing down, as she should be just before being born, Charlotte would not budge. Given the possible complications associated with trying to deliver a baby bottom-first, my doctor told me that she would be scheduling a Caesarean section, which was standard for breech babies.

A week or so later, a woman called me to ask me if I wanted to participate in a study. She said that there was growing concern that an unnecessary number of Caesareans were being performed in cases such as mine so they were looking for women to participate in a study to determine if this was, in fact, the case. With a background in economics and many years of experience in the field of public policy, I know how important it is to have valid numbers to confirm programs or justify changes in policy directions. So in theory, I support the idea of collecting reliable data. However, in this case, it wasn't just an issue of numbers to be studied—it was my life. Therefore, I politely said, "No thank you."

The following week, the same person called me back again to ask me a second time. She said that it was critical that mothers with breech babies agree to participate in the study so that it could be determined, with greater certainty, whether or not Caesareans were actually appropriate in such cases. Again, I said, "No thank you." The person on the other end of the line sounded frustrated with my refusal but just like my unborn baby, I would not budge. I explained that I could understand the need for a study. However, if there were complications when I tried to deliver my baby, to the researchers I would simply be a number. The negative outcome of those complications would be represented by a single digit added to a column indicating that a natural birth had not been a good idea in my case. To me on the other hand, the possibility of being registered in that column meant there would have been serious consequences for my health and most importantly, the health of my baby. I simply could not put my daughter's future at risk in the name of a study.

I didn't think much about that study again until I was pregnant with Mimi a couple of years later. While at my doctor's office for a routine appointment, out of curiosity, I asked a nurse what had become of it. She answered that as far as she knew, the study had proven that it was not a good idea to try natural childbirth with breech babies so they had gone back to scheduling Caesareans in all such cases. I felt sickened when I heard that and validated at the same time. To others, that study was a series of statistics. To me, however, it was the possibility of a terrible outcome that could have affected the rest of my life and my daughter's entire life. Like the chimpanzees, my daughter and I were not just numbers to be studied. We are caring, feeling individuals for whom the potential outcomes could have had profoundly negative consequences. That was my first lesson in following my intuition when it came to the well-being of my daughters. When Charlotte was finally born, safely and without complications, it was the first time I had ever held such a small baby. All I could do was hope that some maternal instinct would quickly develop within me and in the meantime, apply what I had learned from my cat.

From Allie, I had learned about interacting in the absence of verbal communication and the importance of affection and positive reinforcement. I had learned that if you want someone's, or something's attention, it is important to show that you are "listening", even if there are no words being exchanged. If Allie meowed at me, or showed me that she wanted something, I always "answered", either by saying something in response or doing whatever it was that I thought she might be asking for—like opening a door, filling up her bowl or giving her a small piece of the salmon I was eating. I soon realized that Allie varied the sounds she made depending on how she was feeling and what she wanted. A meow in response to me asking her, "Are you hungry?"as I reached for the bag of cat food, was very different from the meow she made if I moved her off my bed when she was looking particularly cozy.

I applied this knowledge to Charlotte when she was about four weeks old. She was sitting in a baby swing in the middle of my kitchen and whenever I came close to her she made what could only be described as "monkey sounds". "Who-who-who... who!" she said. Thinking of my hero Jane, crouching in the woods among the non-verbal chimpanzees, I crouched down in front of Charlotte and repeated the same pattern of monkey sounds that she had made—we are, after all, 98% chimp. As I did, Charlotte's uncoordinated infant limbs moved excitedly as if to show me that she felt validated and thrilled with my response. Then, she made another series of monkey sounds which I also repeated. I continued to respond to Charlotte whenever she communicated with me and she learned to speak at a very early age. As I had done with Allie, I tried hard to make it worth her while to interact with me.

Over the years, I have tried to validate, as much as possible, who she is, what she has to say and who she is to become. I have often thought that Mimi and I are both very lucky that Charlotte was born first. From Charlotte, I learned what the "normal" milestones should be in a baby's development which is the reason I noticed something wasn't quite right with Mimi. Most importantly, from Charlotte, I deepened the trust that I had in my own intuition through the various ways she confirmed it. Ultimately, this combination gave me the minimal confidence and courage required to question what the specialists told me about Mimi's condition and then, follow what my inner conscience was telling me.

– ◆ –

We are 98% chimp, for better or for worse. What we most certainly have, however, is the power to communicate, not just about the present but about the past and the future. The specialist in his lab coat had told me that the brain damage that Mimi had suffered in the past made for a bleak future, so it wasn't worth making an effort to help her in the present. But drawing on my long-ago role models Nancy Drew and Jane, I refused to accept his opinion at face value, no matter how well-informed it might have been. I chose to follow my intuition and I never gave up on my belief that despite the stroke of the past, with a lot of hard work in the present, Mimi's future would undoubtedly be brighter.

Over and over again, Mimi showed me that she was indeed tremendously capable, and it was, in fact, very much "worth the trouble" of helping her. Curiously, as time went on, instead of being told what was not possible, I was increasingly told to keep on doing whatever it was that I was doing because from the point of view of the "experts", progress was definitely being made.

Armed with a sense of purpose, persistence and a profound love for my daughters, I was following my intuition.

3

Setting Clear Goals—
The Briefing Note Approach to Life

The decision to follow my intuition was the first step in figuring out how I was going to help Mimi. I wasn't going to let a guy in a lab coat tell me what my baby could and especially could not do. But as a second step, I needed to put what my intuition was telling me into action. For that, I would need something much more concrete than a "gut feeling". In order to operationalize what I felt I needed to do, I would rely on the lessons learned in my professional life. The two degrees in economics that I completed in my early twenties have been a major factor in enabling me to find work in the public sector. I was first hired for a summer contract when I was working to complete my master's degree. I had no intention of staying beyond that but I did.

What I like about the public service is what it represents—the opportunity to make a meaningful contribution to the wellbeing of others and the intellectual challenge of trying to solve problems that make a difference to people across the country. Governments are highly structured organizations.

You can draw a straight line from the people at the very top who identify the priorities and make all of the final decisions, to any of the people at the very bottom and everyone else in-between. However, a government's day-to-day business is far from linear. The issues are constantly evolving and the way forward can depend on many factors, including the political landscape at any particular point in time, the objectives of individual senior managers and the state of the economy. The result can be a great deal of uncertainty on many levels, constantly changing priorities and a work environment that is unpredictable. Still, in and around all of this there are actually well-established and proven systems that are logical, analytical and effective. One such process is the *briefing note*.

At first glance, this simple document looks unassuming and inconsequential. At a maximum length of one and a half pages, always structured more or less in the same way, with a handful of sections and short paragraphs of no more than five or six lines each, the briefing note could easily be underestimated. However, it is quite possible that each and every government decision that affects all of us in every aspect of our lives, was at one point or another presented to a senior official in such a note. Politicians and priorities come and go, computers become obsolete and are replaced, groups within the bureaucracy are organized, reorganized and then organized back to what they were initially, but the briefing note process endures, largely unchanged.

In essence, briefing notes are the principal means of communicating with the decision-makers at the top of the bureaucracy. In and around the government's day-to-day business, briefing notes provide a snapshot of a situation. They are written in such a way that a busy senior official can quickly and easily understand a complex question and then effectively make an informed decision. For example, sometimes things can go terribly wrong—bridges can collapse, unknown viruses can start to spread or a storm can knock out the power to an entire region. In those moments, the crisis needs to be carefully analyzed, next steps have to be identified, decisions have to be made and actions have to be taken, as quickly as possible. Under such circumstances, briefing notes are an effective means of facilitating a decision. As time goes on, situations are monitored, new developments are taken into account, and updated briefing notes are written and "sent up" the bureaucracy as needed.

— ◆ —

Although it may seem like a bit of a stretch, the briefing note process has been highly relevant to my struggle to help my daughter. Just before I found out that she had suffered a stroke, I thought that my life was relatively under control. Then, all of a sudden I found myself facing a major crisis. It wasn't on the level of a flood or an earthquake affecting thousands of people but it was devastating nonetheless and the impact on my life was massive. I was left wondering, *What does this mean? What should I do next? How will I get through this?* At the time, I obviously didn't sit down and actually write a briefing note on what I should do to deal with the situation. But looking back, I can see that I instinctively applied the same analytical process that I had used countless times when analyzing and providing recommendations on various issues.

The first section of any briefing note is the "issue" statement. In one concise sentence you must clearly outline whatever it is that you need a decision on. All of the information that follows relates to resolving what was set out in the issue statement. Obviously, in any context, clearly defining what it is that you want to achieve goes a long way towards ensuring that you will be successful. In the case of Mimi's stroke, despite what the specialist had told me, despite Mimi's obvious physical limitations and despite my own insecurities, my goal, the "issue" for this virtual briefing note, was that Mimi would be *mainstream by grade one*.

When governments identify a new priority, it is often "big picture". Part of their job is to be visionary and to identify initiatives that could be started now, to benefit large numbers of people in the future, such as new transportation systems, airports and alternative sources of energy. These long-term goals are often massive and most of the time, when they are announced, it is not at all clear how they will be achieved. Still, with a clear vision, a sustained commitment, an appropriate level of investment and a lot of hard work, over time, solutions are found and the vision becomes a reality—which is how we have all of the infrastructure that we currently rely on in our society. A perfect example, is the historic challenge that President John F. Kennedy presented to NASA and the nation, in 1961—to put a man on the moon and return him safely to earth before the end of the 1960s. Now, we are used to advanced technologies in every area of our lives but at the time it was an incredibly ambitious and truly visionary goal. To the average person, it seemed impossible. But by 1969, after an incredible amount of perseverance, creativity, commitment and effort on the part of an enormous number of people, Neil Armstrong's boots actually touched the surface of the moon and the vision became a reality.

In Mimi's case, I knew that I had to do the same thing. I had to aim high. Maybe not as high as the moon but I had to think big. I had to be visionary. If Neil Armstrong's small step on the moon was a giant step for mankind, then surely Mimi's small step, particularly in light of the specialist saying that she would likely never walk, must also be meaningful in some way. In fact, Mimi's small step may not have been a giant step for mankind but it was a giant step for my state of mind. It inspired me to persevere, no matter what anyone told me.

It inspired me to believe that even if Mimi had difficulties in certain areas, incredible things were truly possible.

From my perspective, it was critical that Mimi not be underestimated without giving her a fighting chance. That's why I felt that it was essential to give her the opportunity to start her life as part of the "mainstream". Later on, if it turned out that she couldn't manage, if it was too lofty a goal or if adaptations were needed, I would worry about that then. In the meantime, I had a couple of years to give it my best effort. I would work hard at it and I would adapt as I went along. *Mainstream by grade one* would be my issue statement. It would be my goal, my man-on-the-moon challenge.

After the "issue" statement, the next part of a briefing note is the "background", which explains the context and sets the reader up for the analysis which will follow. The background section of my virtual briefing note was obvious. Mimi had suffered a stroke. I had been told that she would likely never walk, she would probably be developmentally delayed and that from the specialist's point of view, it "wouldn't be worth the trouble" to do anything. However, my background section also included another very important point, which was that I was very committed to helping my daughter as much as I possibly could. That was a major factor in the context of this issue, regardless of whatever anyone else said.

The "analysis" section that then flowed from the background, was that Mimi's mobility was indeed limited and it was possible that she would be developmentally delayed, as the specialist had said. However, with a great deal of effort and motivation, Mimi had learned to walk anyway, even though he had said that she probably would not. This was an encouraging sign which showed promise. And, although it was too early to tell, to me it seemed that at least for the moment, Mimi was learning just fine. I had no specific reason to believe that she was developmentally delayed. So, the conclusion of my analysis section was that despite everything, it was definitely worth the trouble of trying to work towards the goal of *mainstream by grade one*. I had nothing to lose and much to gain.

The last part of my virtual briefing note was to look at what could and should be done–the "next steps". In order to help Mimi, I would need professional assessments and advice. I wasn't necessarily going to follow all of it but it would provide a valuable reference point for all of my actions. Around that time, I was lucky enough to unexpectedly get some good news. Despite the two-year waiting list at the local treatment centre, Mimi was going to get in almost immediately. In all of my frantic calling around, trying to find support for Mimi, I had been lucky enough to reach someone, I don't even know who it was, who, for whatever reason, managed to help me. Perhaps it was just a fluke, perhaps it was the determination or even the desperation that she heard in my voice or perhaps she was just exceptionally compassionate. I don't know what happened but just when I needed to have the guidance of an occupational and physiotherapist, I got a call for Mimi's first appointment.

Between my commitment to helping Mimi and my gratitude for having access to caring professionals who could help me, I made sure to make the most of every minute of every appointment. Every day, I observed Mimi very carefully so that during the appointments, I could explain to the occupational and physiotherapists, exactly what she was doing. I wanted to be able to describe, in detail, the kinds of things that she did and didn't do and the kinds of things that I thought maybe she should or shouldn't be doing. All of the advice they gave me and all of the exercises they suggested became part of my ongoing "analysis" and from that, I identified the steps that I would take to continue working towards my goal.

For example, if a physiotherapist said that Mimi could benefit from jumping on a trampoline to strengthen her legs and stabilize her balance, then I found a place where she could have access to a trampoline. If an occupational therapist said she could benefit from walking on all fours to strengthen her arm and shoulder, then I invented all kinds of games that involved us crawling around on the floor. If I was told that her muscles were too tight for her to do anything with them, then I made sure to gently massage and stretch them as often as I could. I figured that if I kept them from tightening up completely then we could always work on her ability to use them later on. That actually turned out to be one of the more important steps that I took and it facilitated much of Mimi's progress later on.

The drive behind all of my "next steps" was to keep on believing in Mimi, stay focused on the goal of *mainstream by grade one* and work really hard to achieve that goal, for her sake. That was it. That's what I did, one tiny step, one tiny action and one tiny triumph at a time. It was hard, it was frustrating, it was discouraging and sometimes it was heart-breaking but I never gave up on my goal. My daughters matter very, very much to me—nothing else could ever be more important than doing my absolute best to ensure their wellbeing. And so, I continued. To my amazement and to my complete relief, by the time Mimi was three years old it was clear that my efforts were starting to pay off. My goal, as identified in the "issue" statement of my virtual briefing note, was going to be achieved. I knew that I still had a lot of work ahead of me to continue her rehabilitation. I knew that there were still things that she couldn't do and that other consequences of the stroke might still show up later as she grew and developed, but for the moment, my goal had been realized. By following a very logical and structured approach, just like a briefing note, it was becoming clear that Mimi was indeed going to be mainstream by grade one. There was no reason why she wouldn't be able to start school with everyone else.

The key had been to listen to my intuition and then apply a very rational, analytical and practical approach to translating my gut-feeling into tangible actions, which kept me moving towards a very clear goal.

4

Winning the Universal Lottery and Taking Stock of My Life

By about the time I began to realize that my goal of *mainstream by grade one* was becoming a reality, I had another bit of good news. Actually, it was a bit of fantastic, change-your-life-for-the-better news. The outcome of all the medical tests over the last few years was, thankfully and mercifully, that no underlying illness had been found as a possible cause for Mimi's stroke. It had happened, no one could say exactly when or why but it seemed quite certain that it wouldn't happen again.

I clearly remember leaving the hospital after that last appointment. It was early spring. The sky was bright, the sun was shining and I remember noticing, as I stepped out of the hospital, how bright the light was through the budding trees. It had been a short conversation with a doctor following a "heart bubble test". It sounds like such a crazy idea, injecting tiny air bubbles directly into a child's beating heart to see if there are any holes through which the bubbles can escape. If bubbles do escape, it means that blood can also be leaking out of those same holes, leading to a stroke.

I felt like my own heart had almost stopped beating during the test when the doctor, having just stuck a needle into Mimi's chest, said, "Uh-oh..." I didn't have a chance to ask what the problem was because I was already very busy trying not to faint as I watched Mimi's heart on the monitor, wondering how it could even be possible for her to survive such an injection. Thankfully, Mimi did survive, there were no holes in her heart and there were no other potential causes to investigate. The doctor said that what this meant was that there seemed to be "no underlying cause" for Mimi's stroke, and therefore, this was the end of the road for us in terms of medical tests.

That brief conversation was life-changing. The doctor's words looped through my mind. *No underlying cause. No underlying cause. No underlying cause...* Everything seemed so unreal–his words, the intensity of the sun, the buds on the trees, which I was truly surprised to see because I don't think that I had even noticed the seasons changing. I felt weak and at the same time, completely empowered. It was as if I had just miraculously won some kind of universal lottery. As I left the hospital for the last time, I realized that despite all of the painful emotions I had faced over the past three years and all of the horrible potential situations I might have faced had Mimi been chronically ill, the fact was that for us, the worst was behind us. With "no underlying cause", there was no medical reason to be fearful and all that lay ahead was a lot of hard work to help Mimi overcome, as much as possible, the effects of that little dark spot. I had been afraid of the uncertainty but I certainly wasn't afraid of hard work.

In all of the times that I had sat in the various waiting rooms feeling so terrible, wishing that I would wake up from this suffocating nightmare, I had told myself over and over again that if ever, by some miraculous turn of events, I could get out of this situation, if ever Mimi had a chance at a normal life, then I would make the very most of that second chance. I would get my life back on track. I wouldn't be angry about whatever it was that I felt disappointed about right at that moment. I wouldn't resent that I had felt so unsupported and emotionally isolated for such a long time. I would be sincerely grateful for the opportunity and I would make the absolute most of it. All I wanted was a happy and fulfilling family life, for myself, for my husband and most of all, for my daughters. Now, with the extraordinary news that Mimi was not sick and was not likely to suffer another stroke, I had the freedom to try to make that happen.

The first step was to take an honest look at what my life had become. When I stopped to take a good close look, I finally had to acknowledge that my life was a complete disaster area. To start with, we were in a serious financial mess.

- ◆ -

One of the dreams that my husband and I had shared was to combine our professional capacities and work together on something that we both really believed in. For years, we talked endlessly about starting a business with the idea being that even if we worked long hours, at least it would be on our own terms and at least we would be together. I thought that this would be the perfect scenario for us. That way, all of those "very good reasons" that always got in the way would be reasons that were both of ours. They would be reasons that we would deal with together as we raised our children.

We had agreed early on in our relationship that if we ever had children, that one of us would stay home and take care of them until they were old enough to start school. That was part of the commitment to building the kind of family life that we said we both wanted. I would have been happy either staying home or being the one working but it ended up being me who stayed home. After a couple of years, it seemed like the perfect time to start the business that we had talked about, part-time. Charlotte was about a year old and since I was home taking care of her, I spent six months or so working on a business plan. Eventually, we signed a licensing agreement with a company that we were interested in working with and began building our dream.

From the outset, we agreed on two key points, two things that we said were non-negotiable. The first one was that no matter what, we would always put our family first. The second one was that no matter what, we would never mix our personal finances in with the business—*no matter what*. Looking back, it seems rather foolish on my part. I should probably have known better. It didn't take long before the differences in our spending habits that I had noticed when we were first married started applying to the business as well. Of course, right from the beginning we faced the typical challenges and set-backs that often plague new businesses. Some things were much easier than we thought they would be and some things were infinitely more difficult than we could have ever imagined. Because of that, I felt that we needed to move forward very slowly, making sure that we didn't inadvertently do anything that might threaten our financial security and the well-being of our family. But for my husband, it was full steam ahead. "You have to spend money to make money," he would say. I did my best to plug the holes and stem the flow as much as I could but there was a limit to what I could do.

A year or so after we started the business, my husband was laid off from his job. He rejoiced at the opportunity to throw himself into the business full-time. We agreed that if the business did not generate enough income for us to live on once his severance package ran out, then he would go back to working at a salaried job in order to support the family and we would work on the business part-time, until it became more viable.

The months went by, the severance package began to run out, the business was still in its infancy and there were no signs of a willingness to look for a job. I did what I could. I became very thrifty and cut back on our expenses wherever possible. But no matter what I did, my efficiencies were eclipsed by the growing number of "business expenses" that were piling up on our credit cards. I was feeling more and more isolated but whenever I said something to try to slow things down, I was, as usual, being "unreasonable" and "unsupportive". Six months later, the severance package ran out, we had no income and my husband, having had a taste of running his own business, was not prepared to give that up. He wasn't prepared to take care of the girls either so that I could go back to work, he was far too busy for that.

The situation was completely unsustainable and I started to become very anxious. I had so diligently saved for a house in the early years and with my father's help, we had successfully renovated it. I wanted to preserve that hard-earned equity, but how? The solution that I came up with was that we would sell the house to protect the equity and move in with my parents for a few months to remove the immediate pressures. After that, we could review our options—those being that he work and I take care of the girls, that I work and he take care of the girls, or that the business works and we take care of each other. So that's what we did. We sold our house, put our belongings in storage and moved in with my parents, temporarily.

By that time, Charlotte was almost three and Mimi was about six months old. It was shortly after we arrived at my parents' place that I began noticing Mimi's scooching and started to feel that something wasn't quite right. It was around that same time that my husband announced to me one day that he had gone ahead and "invested" the money from our house into the business. I was devastated. It was not his money to "invest" on his own and it was something we had agreed that we wouldn't do.

Not long after that, I had the appointment with the specialist who showed me the little dark spot. So, there I was at my parents' house. I had two young children, one of whom had a serious medical problem that I didn't know how to deal with. I was under suspicion by my doctor for perhaps having caused the mysterious condition and my husband had not only compromised our financial security, but was also so determined to keep working on the business, that he was neither willing to find a job to support the family, nor take the time to attend any of Mimi's appointments.

I felt trapped but as a mother, I felt that I had no choice but to focus on the immediate priority. I needed to figure out how I was going to help my baby. Since I had been told that if Mimi was to make any progress at all, it had to be done within the first two years and, at that point, she was already one year old, I had to do as much as I could in the time that remained. So that's what I focused on—like it or not, the rest would have to wait. And, it wasn't until two years later, when I got the breathtakingly wonderful news that Mimi was not at risk of suffering another stroke, that I finally felt that I had the opportunity to take a close look at my family life and the business. What I saw, along with the financial mess, was a massive emotional mess as well.

When I got back home with the happy news of "no underlying cause", my husband was, as always, too busy to talk to me. In the months that followed, I tried to talk to him about the state of our marriage, about how lonely I felt and how much I wanted to try to get back on track. He was too busy to talk to me then too. In a moment of desperation, I drafted an e-mail to him. I figured that since most of the "very good reasons" that kept him from being able to talk to me originated in his inbox, maybe it would be a way for the girls' and my well-being to make it onto the list of important issues for him to think about.

I asked that we please try to find a solution to the situation that we were in—we needed to find a way to live on our own as a family. I said that I was open to any and all suggestions and that I was willing to go back to work to support us if he were willing to help take care of the girls, at least part-time, and most importantly, help ensure Mimi's continued rehabilitation. I asked that even though he had never been to any of Mimi's appointments, that he please take Mimi to an occupational or physiotherapy appointment, even just once in a while, to at least understand what it was about and to be involved in helping her. I wrote that I loved him and that I wanted to work with him to get things back on track. I pressed send and then I waited. I looked across the room and waited some more. Nothing. No reaction. No acknowledgement. No answer.

When I brought it up later, he said that he was not prepared to address my concerns about our marriage in writing. He thought that was silly. With those words, I felt more isolated than ever before and now, completely without hope. He wouldn't talk to me about the things that were important to me and writing them down was apparently not acceptable either. I was all out of options and I couldn't continue living my life under these circumstances.

— ◆ —

Finding out that Mimi had no underlying illness that might cause her to suffer another stroke was a second chance to parent her "normally", without the painful undertones of chronic illness and fear of what medical problems the future might bring. It was a chance to focus on rebuilding the relationship with my husband and establishing some kind of "normal" family life. The realization, however, that the interest in doing so seemed to be exclusively on my side, brought with it an acceptance, finally, that it wasn't just Mimi's appointments and therapy sessions that I would need to face alone. I would, on my own, have to figure out a way forward for all of the other family-related issues as well. And that's what I did.

5

Facing the New Reality Part I:
Lessons of a Flight Attendant

When I finally accepted that I would be supporting my daughters entirely on my own, I set about trying to get myself some contract work in the government. That's where I had been working before we had started a family and it was the obvious place to start my job search (although it was back in the city that we had left to move in with my parents). I was lucky enough to find work within six months. Even though it was only a 90-day contract and it was a five-hour drive from my parents' place, I took a risk and signed a one-year lease on an apartment, took my belongings out of storage, enrolled the girls in a school and found a day care for them to go to until I finished my work day.

Looking back, I don't know how I found the courage to do what I did based on such a short contract. Then again, I didn't have the luxury of a back-up plan and there was no time for second-guessing. Things had to get done—lunches packed, bills paid, deadlines met, homework finished, laundry folded, appointments made at the treatment centre and rehabilitation activities integrated into our daily routine. I was conscious of the fact that it was a tremendously difficult period in my life but there was no room in the schedule to allow myself to even begin acknowledging and dealing with my own emotional suffering. I needed to stay focused on what needed to get done, sustain my energy and not let the situation that I was in push me to the point of a burn-out. Since there weren't any responsibilities that I could abandon, what was left, was to try to streamline some of them. I started very slowly, making one small change at a time and eventually, over a number of years, developed a system that works for me.

If I had to summarize the approach that I have developed for myself, I would say that it is a distillation of what I learned from my experience working as a flight attendant...

– ◆ –

When I was a child, every summer I would fly with my family to visit my grandparents in Sweden. I was enchanted by the glamorous world of air travel. Everything about it seemed so perfect. Already just stepping onto the airplane felt so fancy and exciting. There was always a beautiful, statuesque flight attendant there to greet us. Ever cheerful and smiling, she always knew exactly where our seats were regardless of how big the aircraft was. I always double-checked my ticket once I got to where she said that we would be sitting but she was right every time. During the safety demonstration, she was calm and in control, inspiring such confidence. She smilingly showed us what we would need to do if there was ever an emergency. Not to worry, in the "unlikely event of a decompression" we would not suffocate because oxygen masks would immediately be dropping down in front of us and all we had to do was simply place the mask over our nose and mouth, and breathe normally. *Breathe normally and trust that everything will be fine.*

In case we ever landed in the ocean, we didn't have to worry either. That fantastic flight attendant had already thought of tucking a life jacket under each and every seat. She was incredible! Then, as the flight progressed and we started to get hungry, she was already on it. While I had been looking out the small round window, playing with the shade and watching everything get smaller and smaller, she had, in that mini-kitchen, somehow managed to prepare a meal for every single person on that plane, without ever getting a spot on that smart-looking uniform of hers. She was thoughtful too. Each dinner tray included a perfect-looking bread roll with its own individually wrapped butter and best of all, there was always a dessert. Oh, how I loved to fly! At the end of the flight, when all of us passengers were looking tired, dishevelled and grumpy, that beautiful flight attendant looked as perfectly groomed and cheerful as when she had first shown us to our seats, which as a child, seemed like a lifetime ago. When I grew up, I wanted to be just as put-together, calm, capable and efficient as those flight attendants.

- ◆ -

Fast-forward fifteen years to when, as a university student, I was hired by a charter airline to work as a flight attendant over the summer. By that time, I had wizened up somewhat to the real world of flying but it still all seemed very glamorous to me. I could picture myself in a stylish dark blue uniform walking through various international airports, following the dashing captain and the rest of the flight crew, with my very own wheeled suitcase trailing along behind me. This was going to be the fulfilment of my childhood dream!

My first reality check came on the first day of flight attendant training. That morning, we were told that over the course of the next five weeks, at least half of us wouldn't make it to the end of the program. When I heard that, I immediately thought, *How hard can it be?* That had long been my standard line to myself in the face of any new challenge. Besides, I had just completed my second year of economics at university and that was the same line that professors always gave us at the beginning of each new semester and somehow, I had always managed to survive to the end. The only flight attendant training exercise that I could even think of was that they might put us on a shaky, elevated platform holding a pot of coffee to simulate turbulence at high altitudes and see if we could successfully serve hot liquids without spilling.

The actual training, however, was in fact much more intense than I had expected. It did not cover serving coffee at high altitudes, mastering the classic flick-of-the-wrist to indicate the location of the emergency exits, safely stowing luggage underneath the seats or putting the tray tables in the locked and upright position. Instead, it focused on safety measures, first aid, evacuation procedures, putting out fires (literally), dealing with difficult situations and learning how the crew worked as a team.

Every aircraft was divided into sections and crew members were assigned specific positions in one of those sections on any given flight. You were responsible for all of the safety equipment in your section and you needed to know exactly where every water shut-off valve, fire extinguisher, emergency locator transmitter and every other type of safety equipment was on all the different kinds of aircraft that the company had in its fleet. You also needed to know what your specific role was in the event of an emergency, in each position and on each type of aircraft. If you didn't correctly answer a mandatory spot question in the crew briefing before the flight, a question which could be related to any of the safety and procedural elements as detailed in your four-inch thick flight attendant manual, you weren't working that day. That was it. There was no flexibility and there was no room for error.

I managed to survive the flight attendant training and at the end of the fifth week, I finally received my fabulous dark-blue uniform and much-coveted suitcase with wheels. I was ready to live my dream! It didn't take me long to realize, however, that working as a flight attendant wasn't nearly as glamorous and effortless as it had looked to me as a child. First of all, you were required to look "flight ready" at all times and the company had a policy of conducting random in-flight assessments. Along with determining whether or not you were appropriately using the chicken-claw metal tongs to pick up ice cubes, rather than scooping them with the plastic cup that you were about to fill (which was far easier than the hard to manoeuvre chicken-claw tongs), a significant part of the evaluation was how "well-groomed" you were. It wasn't too hard to look "flight ready" on departure but as the flight wore on and you started to feel the accumulated effect of dealing with cranky passengers, nausea from the inevitable turbulence and fatigue from working through the night, it became increasingly difficult to maintain the "flight ready" ideal.

In terms of the actual job to be done, you had to work very efficiently. With the arrival time as your deadline, for each flight, every part of the service had to get done and you had to make sure that you fulfilled your particular list of responsibilities. The reality of getting hundreds of greasy meals out of the trolleys in record time was a messy business and that was only the beginning. The clean-up after the meal service was even worse. Random bits of food, cutlery, dirty cups and used napkins hanging off the trays, which never fit as neatly back into the trolleys as they had when you started. You basically just had to shove everything in as best as you could, hoping that you would be able to close the door when you reached the end of your row. There were many times when I thought to myself,

How glamorous am I now in my sweaty polyester suit, with my bloodshot eyes, aching legs and chicken grease from two hundred passenger meals up to my elbows? Not glamorous at all.

Still, there was a job to do, there was no back-up for the duration of the flight and there was no way out until the pilot landed the plane someplace. On top of that, there was almost always something unexpected to be dealt with and dealt with as quickly as possible, so that the passengers didn't notice, which is hard to do in a confined space with no privacy. There were people getting sick, having heart attacks, getting rowdy, smoking where they shouldn't, old ladies losing their dentures, lavatories backing up and overflowing over the Atlantic... You had to maintain your "flight ready" look to inspire confidence, you had to be efficient to get all of your work done and get it done on time, and you had to be prepared, at all times, to respond to any number of emergencies. Once the flight was over and all of the passengers had left, you picked up your suitcase, took a crew bus to your hotel, got a few hours rest and then did it all over again the next day, just as cheerfully and industriously as the day before. This experience prepared me for what I was to face in the future, in ways I could never have expected.

– ◆ –

Clearly, the reality of finding out that my daughter had suffered a stroke is infinitely more significant than what's involved in working on a trans-Atlantic flight. But to me, the overall framework has been applicable. Once I had taken off on this journey, in the sense that I had received the terrible news, there was a lot of work to be done within a short period of time, I had people counting on me to take care of them and looking to me to inspire confidence. I wasn't sure what was going to happen along the way, I had to deal with unexpected turbulence and emergencies, it was often over-whelming, stressful, messy, and tiring but I had to do my best. I had to keep up my stamina, trust that everything would be fine and hope that I'd still be smiling when it was all over.

As superficial as it might sound, the first part of my flight attendant approach to life is the very part of being a flight attendant that I found so uncomfortable—the emphasis on appearance and looking "flight ready". When I first started my life as a single mother, working full-time and taking care of my daughters entirely on my own, I was completely overwhelmed. I was scared and uncertain as to how I was going to pull every-thing together. But it didn't matter how I was feeling, I had everything riding on keeping my job and figuring out how to manage all of my responsibilities. There was no flexibility and there was no room for error, just like when I had been a flight attendant.

The 90-day contract that I had accepted could not be renewed within the same calendar year. Nevertheless, since I had started the job in mid-July, I thought that I would take my chances and hope that the contract would be renewed the fol-lowing January, thereby giving me two contracts worth of time to try to find a longer-term employment solution. In order to make sure that I had the best possible chance at successfully staying employed, I needed to look the part of a professional woman who had everything under control and could deliver solutions to complex projects within tight deadlines as well, if not better, than everyone else. It wasn't an issue of career-building, it was an issue of surviving on my own and making sure that I was taking care of my children. Leaving the house in the mornings looking "flight ready" was essential to project-ing the image of the confident and capable woman that I hoped someone would want to hire within the next six months. Just like when I had been a flight attendant, if I was tired and over-whelmed, nervous or unsure about something, or if something went wrong, it was best that it didn't show on the outside.

At home, a measure of appearing "flight ready" was also important. I needed to inspire confidence in my daughters. I wanted them to feel safe and secure. My reasoning was that if I didn't end up securing a solution to my job situation within six months, then there would be plenty of time for all of us to worry later on. In the meantime, I wanted to give my daughters as good a childhood as I could and that started with showing them that everything was fine, at least as far as they were concerned. In terms of advocating for Mimi, the same principle applied. With all of the negativity that I had to push against, I felt that I would be much more effective if I came across as a mother who believed in her daughter and was confident in her own ability to help her—as opposed to an overwhelmed, tired-looking, hyper-sensitive-pushed-to-the-edge single mother who was barely managing.

As for my own wellbeing, there was no point in looking in the mirror and seeing a haggard version of myself that reminded me of how incredibly difficult this period of my life was. Certainly, this was not the life that I had dreamed of when I was younger or when I had gotten married. Regardless, it was the one that I found myself in at that moment so I had to make the best of it and move forward as best as I could. Apart from my closest friends who knew how much I was truly struggling, I didn't want it to show on the outside to the point where random people would ask, with concern in their eyes, "You're looking tired...are you OK?", or, "You seem a bit off today... is everything alright?" I was by no means OK and everything was far from alright but no matter how well-intentioned those questions were, it was not helpful to hear them and most of all, I didn't want to hear them.

So, a bit of concealer to mask the bags under my eyes, which most of the time felt not so much like bags but like an entire set of luggage, the application of some lipstick and an overall effort to look somewhat "flight ready" went a long way to keeping me on track. As it turns out, there had been a fair amount of wisdom in the airline industry's emphasis on appearance after all.

6

Facing the New Reality Part II:
Preparedness at Single-Mother Altitude

As a flight attendant, once I had arrived at the hangar looking flight ready and participated in the pre-flight briefing, I was then assigned the position that I would be working that day. From that point on, everything about the job was about being systematic and completing the sequence of tasks in the same way every time. You started by making sure that in your section of the plane, there was a life jacket under each and every seat, the safety equipment was securely stowed in its place, all of the supplies that you would be needing for that flight were stocked and the trolleys contained all of the meals that you would be serving. Finding yourself short a life jacket, a meal, a fire extinguisher or any other item at 47,000 feet above the ocean is not an option. Once the airplane has taken off, there is no running out quickly to get whatever it is that you might need—there is no back-up and there is no room for error.

When I first went back to work and started living on my own with my daughters, my situation felt much the same.

Charlotte was six years old and Mimi was not quite four. I had no family in town and I didn't know any of my neighbours. As a result, running a quick errand at the last minute wasn't an option. I couldn't leave the girls by themselves and it wasn't always feasible to take them out with me. Much like in my flight attendant days, there was a requirement for "in-flight preparedness" and being systematic about everything that had to get done. There was a time for checking the supplies and making sure that everything I needed was in its place. There was a time for refuelling and resupplying and then there was a time during which I could not access anything extra. At the everyday-life equivalent of 47,000 feet above the ocean, which as a single-mother is being home alone with your children after dark in the middle of winter, again, there was no back-up and there was not much room for error.

In order to achieve the level of "in-flight preparedness" required under these circumstances, I relied on three things. These three things, or my "time-saving trio" as I like to think of them, have proven to be very effective in making it possible for me to successfully raise my daughters on my own while managing the responsibilities of a full-time job and still have the time required to work towards my daughter's rehabilitation. Equally importantly, this time-saving trio has given me enough clarity of mind to be as creative as has been required to find ways to motivate Mimi to do the exercises that, from her point of view, are boring, frustrating and at times, even painful.

The first element in this trio is...my *toaster oven*. Yes, the often over-looked toaster oven, which isn't even counted as an appliance, is the first item that revolutionized my life towards being able to gain a measure of control over my overwhelming to-do list, and, most importantly, help Mimi overcome the effects of that little dark spot. At that time, every morning I got up at 5:45 a.m. to pack lunches and get the three of us ready for the day. At 8:15 a.m., we left the house and walked two blocks to the school where we waited until the bell rang at 8:30 a.m. As soon as I was certain that the girls were safely inside the school, I walked 1.5 kilometres (about 1 mile) as quickly as I could to my office. It didn't matter what season it was, how much rain was falling, how much snow there was on the ground, or how cold it was with the wind chill factor, I walked to work every single day. There was no back-up and there was no room for error.

Several times a week, over my lunch hour, I walked a total of about 3 kilometres (1.8 miles) to the local shopping centre and back in order to get all of my errands done. There was certainly no flexibility to do any of these things in the evenings when we reached single-mother altitude. If the girls needed shoes, for example, I traced their feet before we left in the morning and tried to choose the right size based on that outline as best as I could. Later that evening, if it turned out that the shoes didn't fit, then I went back to exchange them for another pair during the next day's lunch hour. It was the same thing for their clothes, snowsuits and whatever else they needed. Without a car and with no one to watch the girls, I had to be systematic and creative in how I got everything done.

At the end of the workday, I walked another 2 kilometres (1.2 miles) as quickly as I could to the girls' day care. I picked them up, walked the almost 1 kilometre (0.6 miles) with them back to our apartment and then got started on the evening's activities–preparing dinner, helping them with their homework, doing the laundry and everything else. I had a washing machine in my apartment but there was no dryer, so I had two racks on which I hung everything up to dry. The girls found that their clothes were too "scratchy" when dried this way, so I ended up having to iron most of their clothes to soften them up a bit. It was an enormous amount of work for one person, especially given the emotional upheaval associated with the end of my marriage, the insecurity that I felt about going back to work, the anxiety of figuring out how to live on my own with my daughters and the stress of trying to figure out how to help Mimi. I soon realized that I could not sustain such a level of effort. Enter my trusty toaster oven...

I knew that I could not cut down on my principal responsibilities. So, I started to wonder if there were things I could simply do differently. The Master of Arts in economics that I had completed years earlier had never been of much practical value but the general concept of making efficiency gains became very useful in this situation. Even a small efficiency gain in the evening's routine, as little as fifteen minutes, would represent an advantage from which I could benefit.

As a first step, I thought that I could start by preparing a meal in advance. Then, before picking up the girls from the day care, I could stop in at home to quickly put whatever I had prepared into the toaster oven, and after that, continue on to get the girls. That way, by the time we got back home, we would be able to have dinner right away. On the first day that I did this, the first thing that I noticed as the girls and I walked into the house was the wonderful smell of our dinner, ready to be eaten. It felt so incredibly warm and comforting, as if someone who really cared about me had been working all day to prepare a wholesome meal for the family to enjoy. From that day on, every evening, except Friday, I would stop in at home on the way to the day care and put our dinner into the toaster oven. And, on those nights, as soon as we came home, we sat down to dinner in a house that smelled comforting. In the same way that looking "flight ready" made me feel like I was on track, coming home to the smell of a home-cooked meal (even if it was me who had initially prepared it) made me feel like everything was OK, at least at that moment.

Although the impact of the toaster oven was significant

in and of itself, like in any economic system, I soon bumped up against the limitations of my revolutionary advance. More specifically, since the amount of space in my freezer was limited, so was the range of menu options that I could prepare in advance. The girls liked what I made but when it turned out to be the same three or four items to be chosen from each week, they soon started to complain—a situation which clearly detracted from the advantages of my initial efficiency gains. I realized, that what I needed to do, in order to maximize this efficiency gain, was to expand the number of items to be put into my toaster oven. This led to the second key element in my "time-saving trio"...the *deep freezer*.

That, was revolutionary. All of a sudden, I had lots of freezer space so I could cook and put away as much as I wanted. This was particularly helpful because one of my goals was to make sure that most of our food was organic. A large freezer meant that I could also prepare organic vegetables in the summer for us to have over the winter. The menu possibilities were now endless! I got to work and filled the freezer with soups, pasta sauces, banana bread, muffins and whatever else the girls liked to eat. In the evenings, I took out two containers at a time—one for the thermoses that would be going into the lunch boxes the next day and one for the next evening's dinner. Obviously, now and again I had to take the time to cook large batches of food but it was well worth the effort.

Next, I discovered the third element in my "time-saving trio"...the *slow cooker*. I bought the largest one that I could find. It took no more than 45 minutes to fill and then, for the next six hours or so, while I was doing all sorts of other things, perhaps even outside of the house, the slow cooker was quietly working away in a corner of my kitchen. Again, there was the smell of something warm and comforting when I came home, not to mention many meals to be frozen for another day.

- ◆ -

Between my toaster oven, deep freezer and slow cooker, I managed to achieve the level of "in flight preparedness" that I needed to thrive on my own. This preparedness went a long way to making me feel like I was effectively and efficiently managing all of my various responsibilities. Most importantly, it freed up the valuable time that I needed for other things besides getting the basics done. The time that I have put into my daughter's rehabilitation has come directly from the time that I would otherwise have been standing in my kitchen preparing meals or getting things at the last minute because I was missing a particular ingredient or stressing about ordering pizza because I realized that I didn't have anything in the fridge that night. For the most part, I always knew exactly what I had at home because I was continuously planning and checking. I had lots of food ready to be defrosted at any time, so I knew that I always had something nutritious that we could eat on any given night.

In a discussion about working towards well-being, a naturopath once asked me, "What is the most important ingredient in soup?" I thought of carrots because they are high in beta-carotene, broccoli because it's high in iron, spinach maybe, because it's high in folic acid. I couldn't choose just one ingredient and since I figured it was a trick question anyway, I simply answered that I didn't know. He said that the most important ingredient in soup is *time*. This made a lot of sense to me. As a child, when I had thought that flight attendants could serve up hundreds of meals with virtually no effort, there had already been a massive amount of time invested in order to get those trolleys stuffed with ready-to-be-eaten food. Teams of people had been involved in procuring the ingredients for those meals, preparing them, loading them into the trolleys and then delivering them to the airplane. The most important factor in all of that was *time*. Time had already been invested so when it really counted, when we were 47,000 feet above the ocean, with no access to any other supplies, everything was ready.

Years later, I obviously didn't have entire crews of people to prepare meals for me and my daughters. I didn't even have one person to help me with anything. But all of the food that I prepared and squirrelled away in my deep freezer represented a massive investment of time. The time was there, frozen and ready to be cashed in, whenever I wanted it. That frozen time became the precious ten, fifteen, twenty minutes a day that I needed, particularly on weekday evenings, to do an exercise with Mimi. It was the time that I needed to think about how I could best find new ways of encouraging her to try whatever it was that we needed to work on. It was the time that I needed to give both my daughters the help that they needed with their homework and their music lessons.

Not having to spend precious time and energy planning and preparing food every single evening but still knowing that we were eating healthy meals that I had prepared myself, enabled me to focus on other things. It also gave me a sense that things were under control, even if they weren't exactly. And this, in turn, gave me just enough peace of mind to be as attentive to my daughters as I could be and to be as caring, loving and reassuring a mother as I possibly could be.

As it turned out, working as a flight attendant was not as glamorous as I thought it would be when, as a child, I looked at those beautiful flight attendants with complete admiration. But surprisingly, years later, the experience indirectly gave me a foundation for successfully setting myself up to be effective. Starting the day with an effort to look somewhat "flight ready" went a long way to convincing myself that I was doing fine and that, was the critical first step towards actually being fine. Making sure that I had a certain level of "in-flight preparedness" in my life gave me just enough stability to hold myself together and most importantly, just enough time for the precious rehabilitation activities that have been so critical to helping Mimi develop as much as she has, both physically and emotionally.

And, whenever I started to feel overwhelmed by my responsibilities and suffocated by my stress, just like they said in the safety demonstrations, what I really needed to do was *breathe normally and trust that everything will be fine.*

7

Acknowledging the Accumulated Pain—
After the Turbulence

For the first few years living on my own, there was no room in the schedule to allow myself to acknowledge and deal with my own emotional suffering. From the moment I had put Mimi, with her big smile, into her car seat after that devastating appointment with the specialist, I had stayed numb to my own emotions. Looking back, I think that my unconscious fear was that if I talked about the situation and how difficult it was for me, then maybe I wouldn't be able to maintain the strength I needed to keep going. So many things had to get done and I couldn't let myself get distracted by something so seemingly manageable as my own emotions. I think maybe I was also afraid that if I admitted how painful it all was, then the situation might somehow become cemented into a permanent reality. As long as I stayed focused on what I had to do, there was hope for improvement. Every step forward, no matter how small, was one step further away from a situation that I didn't want us to be in.

I only realized, finally, that I had a lot of pain to be dealt with during a time in which my life had actually become quite stable again. The worst of the emotional and financial turbulence was behind me and my life seemed more "normal" than it had in years. After the first 90-day contract that got me back to work, I had eventually found a permanent job. Two years after that, I had managed to get myself transferred to Montreal, Quebec. One of my goals as a mother was that my children have the opportunity to become fluently bilingual. I thought that living in Montreal, where we could speak both English and French, would be the best solution for us. The transition from an English-speaking province to living and working mostly in French was extremely challenging. However, after two years, we had adapted well. Both of the girls were doing fine in their French-speaking school, the feedback from Mimi's occupational and physiotherapists was mostly encouraging, we had all made new friends and apart from a few bumps along the way, we had settled nicely into our new life.

One of Mimi's biggest achievements was that despite the effects of the stroke and despite the scepticism of those who said it wouldn't be possible, she was learning to play the violin. The violin is a difficult instrument to play at the best of times. On top of that, if you add a hand that doesn't open and an arm that is limited in its mobility, it seems impossible. In all honesty, I wasn't convinced that it would be possible either. But, as usual, I thought that if we didn't try, then we would never know and if we tried really hard, then maybe the tiniest of triumphs might come of it.

To be sure, Mimi's approach to violin playing had to be adapted to her situation. In order to be able to hold the bow, she wore a brace to uncurl her fingers and straighten her wrist which always twisted over to the right. Actually, it wasn't so much that Mimi was holding the bow as it was that the bow was automatically clamped into her hand that closed up by itself anyway. In the beginning, Mimi moved the violin just as much, if not more, than she moved the bow. The result resembled a wide scissor-like movement, which is not at all how the violin is supposed to be played. From my perspective, however, Mimi was managing to get a sound out of the violin regardless of how squeaky and headache-inducing it might have been, and I admired her ingenuity in finding a solution that worked for her.

It certainly wasn't easy, both in terms of how much effort was required by Mimi and how much patience and gentle persistence was required on my part to motivate her. There was a lot of me grinding my teeth and clenching my fists as we spent time trying to figure it out, often followed by some aspirin-taking on my part. Still, after a year and a half of lessons, it was becoming clear that it was actually possible for Mimi to learn to play. And, judging from the concert in which she had, believe it or not, participated at end of that first year, against all the odds, Mimi was playing just as well as the other children her age. It was amazing!

In fact, that year-end concert turned out to be one of the most significant moments of my life. Mimi, smiling and confident, had marched right up to the front of the room and played her song just as well as the other kids. She was beaming. It was abundantly clear that she felt good about herself. Something had indeed come of all the hours of effort, something truly beautiful and it was a significant turning point for me. At that moment, I knew that every minute of effort and every struggle over the past seven years had been well worth it. Despite the heartache, frustration and daily dose of a violin bow grating across the strings of a small, slightly-out-of-tune violin, I felt that I was no longer lost. I was no longer searching for something in the dark. I knew what I had to do and I had proven that it was working. The very fact that Mimi had managed to learn to play the violin at all and then had the confidence to stand in front of a large crowd and play it with her brace on, without feeling self-conscious, was an unbelievable triumph.

- ◆ -

The success of that first year-end concert gave both Mimi and me the inspiration that we needed to keep persevering. Mimi was motivated to keep sawing away at the violin and I was motivated to keep helping her, both in terms of adapting the traditional approach to suit her situation and encouraging her to push herself to overcome the tightness in the affected muscles. Each week I took Mimi to her violin lesson and each week, in-between the lessons, we worked really hard on whatever the teacher had given her to practice.

At some point in the late fall, however, I started noticing that, just like the previous year, Mimi's teacher was always running late by five or ten minutes. And, instead of adding the time to the end of Mimi's lesson, Mimi's lesson always ended right on time. That meant that the students after Mimi were receiving full lessons, while Mimi's was often shorter than it was supposed to be. The first time that it happened I didn't mind too much. The second and third time, however, I started to get a bit irritated and by about the fourth or fifth time I was starting to mind quite a bit. It seemed to me that whenever the violin teacher was running late, she would cut time from Mimi's lesson in order to get back on schedule. For weeks, I said nothing. I didn't want to appear to be the hyper-sensitive-pushed-to-the-edge-single-mother that I sometimes felt like on the inside.

But one day, I felt that the unfairness towards Mimi was too obvious for me to remain silent. That day there was a substitute teacher and the lesson started more or less on time. I left to run an errand. So far, so good. Ten minutes before the lesson was to end, however, I went back to wait for Mimi. I glanced through the window in the door to check on her as I sometimes did. Normally, I would see Mimi playing her violin looking either happy or very concentrated, with her tongue sticking out for good measure. To my great surprise, however, what I saw instead, was Mimi sitting in a chair with her violin case in her lap, looking sad and uncomfortable. Beside her, playing his violin as the teacher looked on, was the young boy whose lesson was before Mimi's. I couldn't believe it! For months I had been noticing that Mimi's lesson was routinely cut short and now, during the half-hour reserved for Mimi, another child was inexplicably being taught while Mimi looked on.

I knocked on the door, opened it and asked the teacher, as calmly as I could, why Mimi was sitting in a chair watching another child being taught when it was her turn. The teacher answered that when the boy had arrived and realized that there was going to be a substitute teacher, he had started to cry. Despite encouragement from his mother, he had refused to stay for his lesson. Apparently, once he had calmed down, his mother had brought him back to apologize, even though by that time, the half-hour reserved for his lesson was over. The mother had nevertheless interrupted Mimi's lesson to have the boy deliver his apology. At that point, it had been decided that in return for apologizing, the boy would receive a partial lesson. But by that time, he had completely missed his own allocated time and it was clearly Mimi's turn.

When I heard the explanation, my inner hyper-sensitive-pushed-to-the-edge single mother self was no longer so inner and I heard myself saying that under no circumstances, when I arrived to pick up my daughter from her lesson, did I ever expect to find another child in her place. The teacher did not agree, arguing that when giving music lessons, it is impossible to maintain a schedule and that parents must therefore remain flexible. I could not have disagreed more. In my teens, I had taught piano part-time, so I knew exactly what was required to keep on schedule when giving music lessons—not very much at all, and certainly no flexibility on the part of parents. If a child arrived late, you taught them what you could in the time that remained of their lesson and reminded them to arrive on time the following week. Out of respect for the students who made an effort to arrive on time, you would always respect the schedule.

So, the next day I faxed a letter to the director of the music school stating that I sincerely appreciated the level of instruction that my daughters were receiving but that I had some concerns about the logistics, as related to their lessons. I politely highlighted my concerns, pointing out that I didn't think that Mimi should be penalized if another child was late, or missed their lesson entirely, for whatever reason. I concluded the letter by stating that I thought that it was important that all parents understand the importance of respecting the established schedule and that I was counting on the director's cooperation to make sure that this type of situation did not occur again.

In response, I received a letter that I found very surprising. The substitute teacher's version of the events was apparently not the same as mine and the director sided with her. Unsatisfied with the result, I decided that perhaps having a conversation with the director would be more effective than a letter. I therefore called her and explained that I still couldn't understand why Mimi's lesson should be given to someone else, under any circumstances. Given that I, like all of the other parents, had signed a detailed contract at the beginning of the year indicating how much I would be paying for 30 minutes of instruction at the same time every week, I expected this to be a straightforward conversation. Again, as in the letter, the director said that she was not prepared to address my concerns. When I asked for an explanation, pointing out the conditions of the contract, she simply said that my concerns "were not important". I kept on trying to resolve the situation but made no progress whatsoever.

Finally, to my complete disbelief, the director explained, calmly and firmly, that my concerns were not important because of what she called the "problem with her hand". *The problem with her hand???* I could not believe what I was hearing. It was true that Mimi had a "problem" with her hand. That was evident because each week she arrived at her lesson wearing a brace that covered her hand and most of her forearm. But what did that have to do with anything in this context? It had been clear to the staff of the music school for the past year and a half, including the director herself, who had been in attendance at the year-end concert, that the "problem" with Mimi's hand was one that we were clearly overcoming, at least in this context. Mimi was playing the violin as well as any other child her age.

In fact, given that Mimi was musical and had developed excellent dexterity in her left hand as a result of always compensating for the right one, she was arguably playing the violin much more in tune than the other children. Therefore, what could the problem with her hand have to do with the length of her lesson and with respecting the fact that in the half-hour reserved for her, she should be the one who received a lesson, not someone else? I felt my face burning with rage. The anguish of the past seven years started to choke me as it formed what felt like a concrete block in my chest. And, seven years worth of uncried tears began to push from behind my eyes, as I realized the implication of what she was saying. She was implying that Mimi deserved less because she was different from the other children.

I couldn't believe it. My goal hadn't ever been to hide Mimi's condition, but rather, to help her overcome it as much as possible and, to the extent possible, make sure that it did not undermine her sense of self. I had done everything that I could to achieve this goal and despite the early prognosis, Mimi was doing surprisingly well. Although that first specialist had said she would likely never walk, she had not only learned to walk, now I couldn't stop her from running everywhere. He had said that she would be developmentally delayed, but so far, Mimi didn't seem to be just developmentally "un-delayed", she was learning in a second language and holding her own at that.

Mimi did have to work much harder than other children but every time a challenge had presented itself, I had worked with her to develop that particular skill as much as possible. There wasn't a teacher or therapist who hadn't remarked on Mimi's tremendous resilience, perseverance and most of all, capacity. It was, in part, the feedback and validation from these teachers and therapists that had consistently encouraged me to continue helping her. I didn't necessarily need any recognition or validation from the director in this case but I did think that a music school that focused on teaching children, might pride itself on its inclusiveness and diversity under such circumstances. Yet here, in the context of something that was, for us, a defining achievement, I was being told that Mimi was "less deserving" because of the very "problem" with her hand that we had worked so hard to overcome.

The director's comments left me reeling. I tried to control my increasingly not so inner hyper-sensitive-pushed-to-the-edge-single-mother self and explain, as calmly as I could, that "the problem with Mimi's hand" had nothing to do with the concerns that I was raising. But she insisted that yes, in fact, it did. I answered to the effect that I did not remember seeing a clause in the contract that I had signed with her, the same as all of the other parents, that stated that a "problem with a hand" would be a factor in the level of instruction that a child would be receiving. Nor had I seen an indication that a child who had a "problem with their behaviour" could randomly bump another child from their lesson. I said that if she believed that Mimi somehow needed less time, for whatever reason, then perhaps it might be more appropriate for us to renegotiate the length of her lesson, rather than just arbitrarily cutting her time as suited the teacher, while I continued to pay for a full lesson. I don't recall what she answered after that, because somewhere at the beginning of the sentence I clearly heard the word "handicapped".

At that moment, the rage that was already burning my face rushed through every part of my body and I could hear nothing but its angry pulse inside my head. No one had ever called Mimi "handicapped" before and I had never actually thought of her as "handicapped". However, in the director's opinion, she clearly was and most importantly, to her it was a legitimate reason for Mimi not receiving the full lesson to which she was entitled. Mimi had been judged as "less able" and was therefore apparently also "less deserving".

That conversation was a watershed for me, figuratively and literally, bringing forth a flood of emotions and tears that I couldn't hold back. In the days that followed, I struggled to contain my feelings as I always had. I tried to push down the rage, break up the concrete block of anguish that had formed in my chest and hold back the flood of uncried tears that was crushing my eyeballs from the inside. But as hard as I tried, I couldn't. I wondered what was wrong with me. After all, I had learned at an early age how to contain my feelings, at least how to control the ones that showed on the outside. But here I was, emotions overwhelming me, completely unable to stop the flow.

At the same time, my analytical self was repeatedly asking why this particular incidence of insensitivity and unfairness was so significant to me. I had long been fearless in standing up for what I believed in, particularly when it came to my daughters. I was normally so resilient and tough. Years ago, a manager had described me as "soft on the outside and a pit bull on the inside". That was a rather accurate assessment—I can be very warm and "soft" and at the same time, incredibly tough at the core when pushed or facing a challenge. But where was that pit bull now? With all that was beautiful in my life, with all that I had overcome to build a wonderful new life for myself and my daughters, with all of the teachers who had been so understanding and kind to us, why was this particular incident of one person's insensitivity all of a sudden hitting me so hard? I just couldn't seem to pull myself together.

The following week, when I took Mimi to her next lesson, I was still struggling with my emotions. This time though, I thought that speaking with the director in person, might bring about some kind of resolution. I thought that she couldn't possibly have meant what she said—surely, there must have been a misunderstanding. When I saw her, I explained that I found it very unfair that a music school, in a community centre that prides itself on community values, was treating my daughter differently because of "the problem with her hand". I said that I found it hurtful that she would call her "handicapped" and use that as a reason for judging her as "less deserving", especially when she was actually proving herself very "able" in this instance. I was certain that she might say something like, "Oh dear, that's not what I meant...When you put it that way, it sounds discriminatory. What I meant to say was...", and then she would fill in the part that would lead to the resolution and mutual understanding. But that is not what happened. Instead, she looked right at me, smiled, shrugged her shoulders, turned around and walked away. It was like being slapped in the face right after having been insulted. Clearly, she had meant it just the way she had said it.

At that point, the floodgates opened and I was drowning in seven years of suppressed emotion.

8

Fighting Discrimination and Sorting Myself Out

W hen I find myself in an uncomfortable situation, I'm not one to sit around idly hoping for a solution to magically appear. I like to think my way through a problem, make a plan and put that plan into action, always moving forward and making adjustments as necessary. Maybe I even find the adrenaline rush of dealing with and overcoming unanticipated challenges somewhat thrilling. But this time, I couldn't see my way past the unexpected flood of emotions. This time, I wasn't able to think my way through it. Thankfully, even in this teary and confused state, a small part of my analytical self was still making itself heard. It was telling me that I was going to have to do something that I rarely did and I certainly didn't like doing. I was going to have to ask for help. Not for Mimi this time, as I had done countless times, but for myself.

In my agenda, was a business card that I had been carrying around for two years. When we first moved to Montreal, the coordinator at Mimi's new rehabilitation centre had given it to me. She said that if I ever needed anything, I could call her. I had confidently answered that I would not, of course, be needing anything. Life was going well for the girls and me. I was independent. Despite my early doubts, I could obviously take care of all of our needs and both girls were doing well in our new life. I was long past needing help with anything, I thought. As it turns out, I was also quite mistaken and the coordinator's gentle insistence on making sure I knew that I could call her if needed, was well-placed on her part. So, two years after that initial conversation, I called the coordinator and asked if I could meet with her. Already that was a big step for me.

The eventual meeting with her proved to be exactly what I needed to get myself refocused and I was profoundly grateful that she had known to be so insistent years earlier. First of all, by coincidence, she too was taking violin lessons so she understood exactly how aggravated I could be by the situation at the music school—both in terms of how disappointing it would be to be consistently given less time than agreed and also, the outrageousness of unexpectedly finding another child in my daughter's place. Already, this validation of my feelings was extremely helpful. After all, my inner hyper-sensitive-pushed-to-the-edge-single-mother self, who had come to the surface through all of this, had brought with her a significant amount of insecurity. In terms of the off-the-charts emotional reaction that I was having, in speaking with the coordinator I realized why it was that I had reacted to the director's comments in the way that I had.

Certainly, there was the element of discrimination towards Mimi that hurt me to the core. But I realized too, that from the moment the specialist had told me about Mimi's condition so many years ago, one of my biggest fears was that she would be discriminated against and how painful that would be for her. In my conversation with the coordinator, I understood that part of my drive to bury my own feelings and work towards making sure that Mimi didn't define herself in terms of her "disability" was that I wanted to protect her from the inevitable meanness that exists in the world. Every step forward that Mimi had made, every activity that she had mastered even though she had done it differently and every tiny achievement that had helped build her sense of self, was one step further away from the likelihood of being treated badly for being "less able". Over time, as Mimi had become more and more capable, I had stopped thinking about that fear because it no longer seemed to be such a significant threat.

When I realized, however, that Mimi was being discriminated against, it was as if the full fatigue of every effort that I had made over the past seven years hit me all at once. At that moment, I lost perspective and felt that it had all been one huge painful waste of time. I had given it absolutely everything that I had, but it hadn't been enough. Even in the context of Mimi's greatest accomplishment so far, she was considered "less worthy" because she was, in the director's opinion, "less able". Talking to the coordinator and understanding why it was that I was so overwhelmed, helped me put things into perspective. I understood why this situation was so painful for me and I realized that what I needed to do was to start by uncovering all of the pain and fear that I had pushed down for so long, release it and allow myself to heal.

But, knowing myself, I also knew that this process would move along much faster if I started by taking on the immediate issue of discrimination against my daughter. After some careful reflection, I decided that I needed a three-part plan, for the short, medium and long-term. Part I of my plan would be to unleash the fierce mama pit bull that my former boss had identified so long ago to fight against the unfairness. Taking control of the situation would go a long way to removing the feeling of being victimized. Hopefully, such action would also work towards changing the attitude of the music school for other children who might be different in some way.

I felt that it was also important to show my daughters that Mimi was by no means "lesser" in any way. It was bad enough that she had had to feel the humiliation of unexpectedly being told to sit quietly and watch as another child received a lesson during her time. But, she had also heard my conversation with the teacher pointing out how inappropriate I had found the situation to be and then later, seen how distraught I had been, despite my best efforts to hide it. I felt very strongly that I had to show Mimi, in no uncertain terms, that we did not accept people treating her as "lesser". I wanted her to know and feel that she had just as much a right to be at that music school and to have a full lesson as every other child—with or without her brace, with or without a little dark spot somewhere on a blurry picture.

Once I had accomplished that, I would move to Part II of the plan, which would be to work out the rest of my raw, unresolved feelings more openly and thoughtfully. I figured that there was probably more where that flood of emotion had come from. Finally, Part III, to be realized over the longer-term, would be to one day do something constructive with what I had learned, like maybe writing a book...

Starting with Part I of the plan, I stayed up all night researching the laws that protect against discrimination. Following my usual briefing note approach to life, I set myself a clear goal—a very bold issue statement indeed. I was going to fight the discrimination head-on. Next, in true briefing note fashion, I needed to make sure that my virtual background, analysis and next steps sections were structured so that I would have the greatest possible chance at succeeding in what I had set out to do. With my approach fully structured, I sat down and very carefully crafted a letter addressed to the director of the music school.

I started the letter by thanking her for having taken the time to respond to my first letter. I continued by saying that I disagreed with the version of events as she had outlined them in her written response, but, in fact, what I found most disturbing, were the judgements that she had expressed in the course of our conversations. I said that, to be more specific, I didn't understand the relevance of raising Mimi's so-called "handicap" when the situation in question did not, in fact, personally concern my child at all. Rather, it was simply a logistical concern related to the way in which the school was being managed. I went on to ask if, in her capacity as a manager of a music school, she was actually even in a position to judge whether a child is "handicapped" or not. Furthermore, from the point of view of Mimi's musical training, I asked if it was really appropriate for her to be to judging my daughter as "handicapped" at all. I pointed out that yes, Mimi does wear a brace and yes, she does play the violin in a way that is, perhaps, a bit different from the other children. However, each week Mimi arrives fully prepared for her lesson and even participated in the year-end concert with as much success as the other students her age.

Then, I pointed out that the music school must surely support the principle that all children be treated in a way that is free from judgement and discrimination. I suggested that her reference to a so-called "handicap", as a justification for refusing to acknowledge my concerns related to logistical considerations, was a clear demonstration to the contrary. I closed the letter by saying that I presumed that she was aware of the legislative frameworks that protect children against judgement and discrimination. And, if not, I would invite her to look them up before our next exchange. In closing, I offered her my best regards and signed off.

I worked and re-worked the letter with input from my family and close friends to make sure that it was as streamlined and as sharp as a deadly arrow. I wanted to hit the discrimination squarely in the heart with one swift blow but I wanted it to glide in as gracefully as possible. Once I was comfortable with the wording, I sent it by registered mail. I did this for two reasons. First of all, I wanted to make sure that I could confirm whether or not the letter had indeed arrived in case I was going to have to go further along in my list of potential "next steps". At that point, I had decided that I was prepared to go as far as required to make sure that no other family would ever face the same kind of treatment by that music school. Secondly, I wanted to make the seriousness of my intent very clear. Nothing says "this is serious" like a registered letter. If the director had judged me by my soft single-mother exterior then she was about to feel the presence of a mama pit bull that had been seriously disturbed.

The following week I took Mimi to her violin lesson as usual. When the director saw us, she went into her office and came out holding an envelope. It was another letter, but this time, it was not written on the school's letterhead. Just looking at her, I could see that her body language was at the opposite end of the spectrum from the day that she had indifferently shrugged her shoulders and walked away, as I tried to open a dialogue on how hurtful and inappropriate I had found her words to be. As she gave me the letter, I thought that she looked kinder somehow, as if she had perhaps taken some time to reflect on the situation since the last time we had spoken. Her letter started by saying that there seemed to have been a "misunderstanding". This was the resolution that I had been looking for. She wrote that if she had chosen words that had "shocked" me, then she sincerely apologized, having perhaps, "involuntarily" chosen an "inadequate general term". This of course, did not explain the fact that there had clearly been no "misunderstanding" when she had shrugged her shoulders and walked away but at least it was a direct acknowledgement of the fact that the situation had indeed been inappropriate. I believe that seeing her own words reflected back to her on paper as they really were, discriminatory, and seeing them in the context of the kinds of legal frameworks that we have in our society to guard against this type of attitude, was enough to set things straight.

As I read her letter, I felt the mama pit bull receding back into the quiet inner place where she normally sleeps, undisturbed until awakened by some outrage. Part I of the plan had been a success. Although I had been prepared to go much further, I was happy that the situation had been effectively resolved with one more carefully researched and crafted letter. I had the sense of resolution that I needed and I no longer felt that Mimi and I were somehow victimized. The sleepless night preparing the letter had been well worth it and I knew that in the future, I would not hesitate to stand up for what I believe in.

I was grateful that I had found the courage to ask for help from the coordinator and most importantly, that I had had the good fortune to receive exactly the support that I needed, when I needed it the most. As time went on, in some peculiar way I almost felt a strange sense of quiet gratitude towards the director of the music school. Not that she had been so hurtful, of course. Rather, that in some back-handed way, the hurtfulness of her words had forced me to deal with a fear that I had hidden away from myself for many years and tried so hard to ignore.

After this major resolution, I was ready for Part II of my plan—uncovering and dealing with what was left of the hurt. For me, that involved a lot of reading on grief and grieving, talking to my friends more openly and, through the coordinator, befriending a mother whose daughter had also suffered a pediatric stroke but who was ten years older than Mimi. My new friend's openness in sharing her experience with me went a long way to making me feel less isolated, more secure in my own journey, more hopeful and more empowered to keep on persevering.

This, of course, brought me directly to Part III of my plan—sharing my own experience in the hopes that it too, in turn, could be helpful to someone else.

9

Breathing Normally—
Inspiration from the Goldberg Variations

In the early years on my own, while the toaster oven plan was in effect from Monday to Thursday, Friday nights were different. In order to make sure that we were always "fully refuelled before take-off", on Friday nights, before picking up the girls from the day care, I would stop by the grocery store to buy everything that I needed for the coming week. Because I didn't have a car, I arranged for the groceries to be delivered and noted that if I wasn't home, everything could be left on my front porch. As the groceries were making their way to my place, I was on my way to the day care to pick up my beloved daughters. That was always, by far, the best part of my day. I was truly happy to see them each and every evening, and they, ever loving and affectionate, always looked so happy to see me too—much like the many boisterous, hug-filled reunions that I had seen at the airports in my days as a flight attendant. After packing up the girls' knapsacks and helping them with their coats, it was time for us to walk home.

Because I had stopped for groceries on the way to the

day care rather than going home to put something into the toaster oven, on Friday nights there was no warm and inviting smell when we got home. Instead, I would start the evening by bringing in and putting away everything that had been delivered, and then, make a quick dinner. By about 7:00 p.m., between my battle with that week's to-do list and the associated 25 to 35 kilometres (16 to 22 miles) that I had walked over the last five days, my inner batteries were completely depleted.

As a result, I started what we called our "music nights". Every Friday night after dinner, we would brush our teeth and put on our pyjamas. We would go into the living room and lay pillows and blankets down on the carpet. I would light some tea lights and turn off the ceiling lights so that the room would look cozy. Finally, I would put on some classical music. The three of us would lie down on the carpet together, listen to the music and "cozy-up" as the girls liked to called it. For the first while, we would talk about whatever four and six year-old girls like to talk about with their mother, along the lines of...*Mama, what makes play dough smell so funny? Mama, is it better to finger paint with one finger or the whole hand? Mama, can you pack popsicles in a lunch box? Mama, how much love does a mama have for her girls?* (To the end of the universe and back...) Eventually, when all of the questions had been answered and the girls were feeling especially cozy and safe, they would fall asleep and I would be alone with my thoughts—and there were plenty of them competing to keep me company.

My mind would be racing, trying to sort through all of the unresolved, conflicting and overlapping emotions that were knotted up together in my head and my heart would still be pounding from the adrenaline-fuelled exertion of the week. I was relieved to have gotten through another week, to be lying peacefully all "cozied-up" with my daughters and at the same time I was extremely anxious about our future.

Without a secure full-time job and no support from their father, I wondered what was to become of us three girls out in the world on our own. I felt hesitantly triumphant that I had gotten this far and that I had managed to make sure the girls and I were alright for the moment. But along with that, I felt insecure about my ability to maintain what I had started. I was cautiously optimistic that if I continued to work hard, I would be able to take care of us but at the same time, I was so very afraid that, for whatever reason, maybe hard work wouldn't be enough.

I was proud of myself for having had the strength to get out of a marriage in which I had ultimately found myself alone, isolated, shouldering all of the responsibilities for our children and so chronically lonely. But now, I really was very much alone, isolated and shouldering all of the responsibilities for our children. Strangely, the difference was that now, I was no longer lonely. The loneliness had come from years of unfulfilled expectation. It had come from waiting to feel that the person to whom I had made a life-long commitment cared enough about me to ask me how I was doing from time to time, cared enough to listen when I said that I wasn't doing well and most of all, cared enough about the girls and me to want to spend time with us and maybe even take care of us a little. Now, out of the marriage, there was, of course, no longer the expectation that someone would do any such thing. I knew that there was no one to help me. There was no one to share in the responsibilities or even the joys of raising the girls. There was no one to share in the decisions about their well-being or reassure me during the times when it all felt so overwhelming. Now, I really was alone.

I felt a tremendous sense of sadness and failure over the fact that the marriage had been such a calamity. Nevertheless, there was some small comfort in the fact that the conditions for loneliness were no longer part of the picture. As I lay there on the carpet with my girls sleeping next to me, my mind a tangled mess of unresolved emotions, I found it comforting to listen to my favourite pieces of music. My absolute favourite recording and the one that we listened to on most Friday nights, is Johann Sebastian Bach's Goldberg Variations as recorded by Glenn Gould.

— ◆ —

The Goldberg Variations were written by Bach in 1741 at the request of a Russian count. Legend has it that Count Kaiserling, unwell and suffering from insomnia, commissioned Bach to compose something for him that would be "soothing and cheerful" and could be played for him whenever he couldn't sleep. In exchange for a golden goblet full of coins, Bach wrote the Goldberg Variations, named after the Count's personal musician Johann Gottlieb Goldberg who was the person called upon to play for the Count in the middle of the night. The title page of the published score reads, in German, "...composed for connoisseurs, for the refreshment of their spirits..." It is said that the Count did indeed find the variations soothing and refreshing, and that he never got tired of hearing them on his sleepless nights.

The Variations consist of an "opening number" called the aria, followed by thirty variations of that same aria and finally, the initial aria repeated one more time as the "closing number". Even when they were first written, the Variations were considered incredibly creative and innovative. Rather than base them on the melody, as is most often done, Bach used the bass line as the starting point. As a result, it is not easy to hear how the variations are linked to the opening theme since it is much easier to follow variations that are based on a melody. But, there is indeed a direct, mathematical link from each of Goldberg's variations back to that opening aria.

What I love about the Goldberg Variations, especially as played by Glenn Gould, is that for me, one by one they reflect just about every possible shade on the spectrum of human emotions. After the slow, contemplative aria at the beginning, the first variation sounds nostalgic and tender, and from there, the music reflects sadness, lightheartedness, cheerfulness, exuberance, wistfulness, anger and everything in-between. With the repetition of the aria at the end, albeit a little more slowly than the first time, there is a feeling of resolution, familiarity and closure.

Much like the Variations themselves, Glenn Gould was also known for his creativity and innovation. At the age of three he was already reading music and by five, he was creating his own compositions. By the time he was 22, Gould was ready to make his first recording and the music that he chose was the Goldberg Variations. With his unusual mannerisms, tendency to sing along while he played, requirement to have the room at exactly the right temperature, the piano at just the right height and only his own lucky chair to sit on, Gould was considered eccentric. Eccentric or not, his first recording was a huge success, being called one of the century's greatest recordings.

It is said that the conductor George Szell, who led Gould in 1957 with the Cleveland Orchestra, once remarked, "That nut's a genius". Perhaps he was a bit of a nut. But, with his insistence on interpreting the music in his own, inspired way, Gould pushed the boundaries of creativity and innovation further than anyone else. In doing so, he achieved a level of technicality and musicality that was unparalleled.

A quarter of a century or so after his first recording, Gould decided to re-record the Goldberg Variations in the same New York studio as before. In contrast to the first recording, however, which was highly energetic, the second time around Gould approached the Variations somewhat differently, playing them much more slowly and reflectively. Over the years, he had worked out an ingenious way of interpreting the Variations as one cohesive piece of music rather than a series of individual pieces, as they were normally played. What Gould did, was that regardless of how each variation was written and regardless of the mood that each one reflected, he found a way to keep more or less the same rhythm from the very beginning right through to the end. In essence, he created a steady pulse that beats through the entire recording. It is this second recording that became the feature of our Friday evening "music nights".

At that time, I didn't know the history of the Goldberg Variations and I didn't know that they had been written to "soothe the spirits" of someone who had had trouble sleeping hundreds of years ago. But strangely enough, as I lay there on the carpet in my candle-lit living room with my girls, that's exactly what they were doing. As soon as the opening aria began, I felt my breathing deepen, I started to relax a little and I felt my heart rate slowing down from its accelerated adrenaline-induced pounding to a more natural pace, inspired somehow by the steady rhythm set by Gould in that ancient opening number.

As I listened to the variations and to the emotions that each one reflected, it was as if, one by one, my own emotions were being taken out of the stormy, swirling middle of my mind and placed carefully on their own, somewhere in the periphery, no longer mixed up with the others. The anger was no longer mixed up with the happiness, the fear was no longer with the hope, the insecurity was no longer with the sense of accomplishment and the anxiety was no longer mixed up with the sense of relief. I could start to breathe normally and trust that everything would be fine. By the end of the thirty variations, with all of my emotions successfully untangled from one another and safely stowed away in separate compartments, my mind felt clear and organized. The final repetition of the aria, signalling the end of the variations, brought with it a sense of closure for me also and soon, I too was asleep.

The "music nights" had started out as a desperate coping mechanism on my part, a way to deal with my inability to muster up even the tiniest bit of energy at the end of another stressful week. They were a reaction to a state of complete exhaustion but ultimately, served to nurture my strength and well-being.

10

Rehabilitation—
Piano Lessons and More Variations

In-between the music nights, I would sometimes listen to that same recording of the Goldberg Variations as I walked the seemingly endless school-work-day care circuit. As I walked along, letting the music organize my thoughts for me, I would sometimes daydream about how my life might be many years in the future. That is, after my current situation would have long since been stabilized, after I would have done absolutely everything that I could to help Mimi and after the girls were grown and leading happy, productive lives. I would picture myself in a small cabin somewhere on the edge of a lake. I would have a piano, a coffee maker, a copy of the Goldberg Variations and nothing to do all day but dedicate myself to learning how to play that beautiful aria and all of its extraordinary variations.

Growing up, I had the privilege of many years of piano lessons. Although it's clear that no amount of determination on my part would ever enable me to play the Variations like the brilliant Glenn Gould, I know that even without ever taking another lesson, I have enough knowledge of music and enough of a foundation to sit down and learn to play them. What would be required, if I ever do find myself in a small cabin on a lake with a piano and nothing else to do, is patience and a whole lot of time. I know this because I have been on both the giving and receiving end of piano lessons, including successfully guiding Charlotte through her process of learning to play the piano. I know that the most important part of learning to play a piece of music, be it the Goldberg Variations or the most basic beginner piece, is not so much the teacher that you have, how long your lessons are, how long you have been taking lessons or how talented you might be. What is required, is a combination of factors, the most important of which is a sustained personal commitment, or in the case of a child, a sustained personal commitment on the part of a parent.

First of all, you obviously need some basic instructions in order to understand what it is you're supposed to do—that's what the lessons are for. But once you have those instructions, you need to take the time to really understand what they mean and most importantly, how they apply to what you want to achieve. Then, you need to develop the physical capacity to actually apply the instructions and begin learning to play something on the piano. In the beginning, this task may seem virtually impossible. Most people's fingers don't naturally move as fluidly and independently as is required to play the piano. Furthermore, the instructions, which may already have seemed vague during the lesson, can seem even more so after the lesson, as you stare at the complex notation on the page in front of you and try to somehow make the link with your clumsy fingers. It is natural to feel discouraged at this point and question if it is even worth the trouble of going through with it all. It is also natural to find yourself entertaining the idea of abandoning the entire process because trying seems so futile. This is where the personal commitment comes in.

In order to learn to play the piano, you need to be patient. I have had so much trouble being patient in my life that at one point, I actually looked it up in the dictionary in an effort to understand what it truly means and why I have always had so much difficulty with it. *Patience* comes from the Latin word "pati" which means *to suffer*. That explains everything. In trying to achieve "patience" I have felt an enormous amount of "pati", only to find out that the "pati" or "suffering" is inherent to the very state of being patient! But that is exactly how it is. Learning to play the piano requires a tremendous amount of patience–suffering through the frustration of trying really hard but not seeing any results right away and feeling the discomfort of facing the unknown. Along with that difficult-to-achieve patience, you also need a lot of perseverance. You need to continue your efforts even when you don't feel like you are making progress and you feel that your patience is, in fact, wearing thin—which again, of course, involves feeling a whole lot of uncomfortable "pati"...

However, though you may not see, feel or hear the difference, every minute that you spend trying is a quiet investment in your own ability and one day, you are very likely to surprise yourself. It may be just a tiny accomplishment, imperceptible to everyone else. But you will know what you couldn't do at the outset and you alone will know how far you have come. So, although the actual piano lessons are important, learning to play the piano hinges mostly on what you do with your time *in-between* the lessons. It is your personal commitment to being patient and to putting in the time to learn, even in the face of a lot of "pati", that will make the difference and determine whether or not you will actually ever learn to play.

In my case, I'm not sure that I will ever find myself in a cabin with nothing to do but learn my favourite piece of music. But, in the meantime, I have made good use of this knowledge in the context of my daughter's rehabilitation.

– ◆ –

When we are sick or when something goes wrong, we have a tendency to want someone to fix it for us. We want a pill, an operation or some other quick solution to make whatever it is go away. Unfortunately, that is not always possible. As a second-best solution, when there is no pill or operation, we want regularly scheduled appointments for some kind of treatment, any kind of treatment, that, even if it takes a long time, will eventually still make the problem go away. When I found out that Mimi had suffered a stroke, it was clear that there would be no pill or operation that could make it go away or reverse the effects of that little dark spot. So, as a second-best solution, once I realized the value of occupational and physiotherapy, I thought that a series of regular treatments would be the way to "fix" the problem, as much as possible. I could picture several intense years filled with many appointments during which I would look on from the sidelines, as the caring and capable professionals worked with Mimi to help rehabilitate her affected limbs.

It was with great anticipation and hope that I got us ready for our first appointment at the rehabilitation centre. When we got there, the first thing I noticed was the cheerful décor and pleasant staff at the reception. So far, so good. But once I sat down and looked around the waiting room, what I noticed most of all was the utterly bleak look in the eyes of the other parents waiting with their children. It was a look that seemed to communicate a complete lack of hope—a sense of emotional devastation, defeat and discouragement. I had trouble reconciling what I was seeing with the optimism that I myself was feeling, given that I was so happy to be in the very place where I was going to get help for my daughter. Not to mention, the complete gratitude I felt for even having been accepted to come in at all.

Truth be told, those first appointments turned out to be very discouraging and I started to understand what it was that I was seeing in the faces of the other parents. As wonderful as the occupational and physiotherapists were, the advice that they were giving me seemed vague and trivial. The exercises and activities that I was supposed to do with Mimi seemed rudimentary and, dare I say, irrelevant, to the goal of Mimi being able to move her limbs and hand better. The rigid braces they were recommending for her delicate hand and leg seemed so severe that I couldn't imagine torturing my little Mimi with such terribly restrictive devices. Besides, the appointments were so few and far between that I couldn't see how they could possibly lead to any progress at all, let alone any kind of "fix" over time. As a result, despite the optimism and gratitude that I had felt walking through the front door of the treatment centre that first day, I soon began to feel as if my own eyes were well on their way to communicating something bleak as well. I felt a growing sense of despair as I wondered how these few appointments, basic exercises and torturous braces could possibly help Mimi get better.

My analytical mind turned the problem over and over again and, at some point, it occurred to me that maybe I was looking at the situation the wrong way round. Instead of seeing the visits to the rehabilitation centre as the time during which a professional would be helping Mimi to make progress, I started seeing them much in the same way as I had my piano lessons. Mimi's appointments were not the time during which most of the learning and progress would be made. I would not be sitting comfortably on the sidelines while someone else provided an effective "fix" to the problem. Rather, the appointments were an opportunity to get the basic information and instructions that I needed to understand Mimi's situation and figure out what it was that I could do to help her. The actual learning and progress that she was going to be making would be occurring *in-between* her appointments. What was required, just like with the piano lessons, was for me to make a personal commitment, be patient and put in a whole lot of time.

Just like with my piano lessons, at first the task seemed almost impossible. I felt overwhelmed by what had to be done and by how slow the progress was—if I even saw any progress at all. It all seemed so insurmountable. But, just like it had been with my piano lessons, even though at first there seemed to be little, if any, progress, slowly, slowly, slowly, one tiny step at a time, I started to notice very small improvements. They were perhaps imperceptible to anyone else but me (and Mimi's occupational and physiotherapists, of course) but the improvements were there nonetheless.

What I realized, was that the key was for me to take on the responsibility for Mimi's rehabilitation myself. I had to become the expert on how she was doing. Maybe I couldn't explain her situation in the appropriate medical and technical terms but I observed everything that she did and how she did it. When it was time for her next appointment, I didn't just wait for advice, I explained what I saw and what I thought that she might need. If I didn't agree with the answer, for example, on the many occasions that I was told that Mimi could progress no further, then I kept on persevering. I asked, "What if it *were* possible, what would I do then?" If I didn't get an answer that I could work with, then I would phrase my question differently, asking instead, "What is it *specifically* that is preventing her from progressing further?" If the answer to that question was muscle tightness, then I would spend time in-between the appointments massaging those particular muscles, stretching them and moving them as they might have moved if Mimi had been able to use them. If it was an issue of the connection between her hand and her brain, then I found other ways of encouraging Mimi to try anyway. We are told that the brain is plastic and that it can rewire itself after an injury. My question to myself then was...*Well, if that's the case, then why on earth would that not be applicable to Mimi as well?*

When I was child, I had a friend who could raise one eyebrow. I thought her ability to communicate attitude with that raised eyebrow, without saying anything at all to get herself into trouble, was the absolute best thing I had ever seen. I sat in front of the mirror in my bedroom for hours until I finally learned to do it too. It was a muscle that I didn't know I had a use for and I didn't know how to get it to work but I was motivated. I believed that it was possible and so, eventually, I learned to use it. If I could learn to use a miscellaneous eyebrow muscle then surely Mimi could learn to use some of the muscles in her hand. My conviction was that there was absolutely no reason why Mimi couldn't regain at least *some* of the capacity that she otherwise would have had were it not for that little dark spot. She was young, she has all of the muscles, all of the bones, all of the nerves and everything else that makes up a hand. And, she has a brain that is clearly functioning as it should. There would be no accepting "she can progress no further" without a whole lot of effort and patience sustained over a whole lot of time.

And finally, again from my experience learning to play the piano, I ultimately realized that patience and time on their own were not enough. If I truly wanted to help Mimi, then I also had to find a way to be creative and innovative even through all of my own "pati". Restricting myself to the instructions and activities that I received during the appointments with the occupational and physiotherapists, meant that Mimi's progress was limited. She quickly became bored with whatever it was that we were supposed to be doing and I became frustrated. Instead, taking my inspiration from the Goldberg Variations, I started looking at the information that I got from the appointments as the "aria"—the theme or starting point upon which I would create dozens and dozens of variations for Mimi. And create variations I did. Whether it was inventing one-time games, playing with finger puppets, digging in the sand, taking her to a new play structure, encouraging her with treats, distracting her with unexpected silliness and ridiculous sounds, constantly encouraging activities that require two hands—like sewing, riding a scooter and eventually, playing the violin—I took the basic elements of whatever theme we were given during the appointments and I turned them into countless variations.

As with the Goldberg Variations, based on the bass line rather than the easier to follow melody, the underlying themes of my variations were not always apparent either, especially to Mimi. But they were always there. Each of my variations had a link with whatever it was that we were trying to accomplish. It wasn't necessarily a major effort every day either. I was, after all, busy trying to hold everything else together at the same time and Charlotte too needed love, attention and caring, of course. But, whenever I saw an opportunity to integrate a theme into our daily routine, then that's what I did. The key was constantly showing Mimi that there was indeed a use for that "other" hand and setting her up so that she would increasingly use it, at least as a "helper hand". Obviously, Mimi couldn't always do things exactly like everyone else. But my own theme, the one upon which all of my other variations were based, was that if I could show Mimi that her right hand could indeed be useful to her and that she could, if she worked at it, increase the use of that hand, then she would continue to make progress.

The variations on this theme continuously brought wonderfully encouraging signs of improvement. As soon as Mimi learned something new, as soon as her muscles were even just a little bit less tight than before and she had even just a little bit more dexterity than before, then I could see that she automatically integrated that functionality into all of her activities. And, the more that she spontaneously used that hand, even marginally, the more she continued to develop its strength and usefulness to her. As it had been with the piano lessons, Mimi's progress wasn't necessarily apparent to anyone else. But I knew how limited her movement had been at the outset. I knew how valuable even the smallest improvement was and what a triumph each step forward really was.

Like my favourite recording of the Goldberg Variations, the repetition of this theme and all of its glorious variations as played out in the activities of our daily routine over the years, served to nurture my strength and optimism. It continuously reinforced my personal commitment to persevere and help my daughter with as much patience and time as I could possibly give.

11

Finding Reasons to Persevere— My Collection of Fireflies

Making a personal commitment to help Mimi overcome the effects of the stroke was relatively easy. I believed in her and I wanted her to have the best possible start in life. The hard part was sustaining my patience and then translating that patience into the perseverance required to help her over the longer-term. That part didn't just come on its own. It was something that I had to foster and nourish somehow. In a context that was predominantly negative, in which I was, on an ongoing basis, told what was not possible and what could never be, there wasn't much to go on. Regardless, in the same way that I had turned the slight element of doubt in the specialist's own words into a reason to persevere, I was constantly searching for small signs that might indicate that something positive might be possible. I was always on the look-out for little flickers of hope that could foster my belief in Mimi's capacity and nurture my drive to keep persevering, however fleeting and intangible those little flickers might be.

It was a bit like my experience catching fireflies on a high school camping trip many years before. Sometime in the late spring, we packed our knapsacks, left our boat shoes behind and travelled out of the suburbs to spend a few days in the wilderness. During the day, we hiked through the woods and in the evenings, the older kids organized activities to keep us entertained. One evening, the featured activity was a game they called "making a flashlight". Each of us was given a clear plastic bag and told to go off and collect as many fireflies as we could. At the end, the person whose bag glowed the brightest would win the game. We weren't given a lot of time, however, so most of us just ran around wildly in the dark grasping at whatever we could until someone yelled, "Stop!"

The thing about fireflies, is that they don't glow very brightly and they don't necessarily glow consistently either. They flicker here and there as they go about their quiet bug lives. Just because you don't see them, however, doesn't mean that they're not there. Maybe, at the exact moment that there was a little flicker of light, you just happened to be looking the other way. Maybe, there was some deadwood in the way so that you didn't even have a chance to see the flickering. Or maybe, you were just too distracted by the fact that you were racing around to even notice. That's how it has been for me as I've looked for little flickers of hope and tried to make my way through the dark, trying to figure out how to help Mimi. It would have been easier, of course, if along with her diagnosis, I had been handed a glowing bag of fireflies, so to speak, to guide me and serve as a constant source of inspiration. But unfortunately, that's not how it works. Each person is responsible for finding their own little flickers of hope and keeping their own collection glowing within themselves as they travel along facing life's challenges.

In my case, I found that the key was keeping my eyes and my heart open as much as I possibly could. Just like the fireflies, the fleeting signs of hope were all around me but they were not necessarily obvious. For example, when Mimi was a baby, I was always carrying her around on my hip. Every time that I opened the fridge she would put her finger to her mouth and make a sucking sound. At first, I didn't think much of it since most children have at least one finger in their mouth at any given time. But, when Mimi pointed to the drink box in the fridge and then sucked on her finger as she would a straw, I realized that she was trying to tell me something. She wanted me to pass her the drink box. I did and she smiled widely. I interpreted the fact that she had figured out a logical way to communicate what she wanted as a little flicker of hope and officially started my inner collection of firefly light.

The following year, I was lucky enough to find a particularly bright flicker of hope. Right from the beginning, I had felt that I needed to help Mimi understand that even though her right arm tended to stay curled up at her side and her right hand was always closed-up tight, that she did, in fact, have a use for them. An adult who has suffered a stroke knows how useful their affected limb was to them before the stroke, so afterwards, they know exactly what they are working towards and why they are trying to regain the ability that the stroke took away. Most importantly, their memory of the capacity that they had, is a very strong motivator. The difference with pediatric strokes on the other hand, is that babies have no memory of ever having been able to use the affected limbs. They don't know what is possible so they have no motivation to try. Their baseline, or "normal", is that one side of their body is limited in its range of motion. And, because they are still babies, you can't explain to them what has happened or why they should at least try. So, in Mimi's case, I went back to what I had learned from Allie. I was going to have to show Mimi what she needed to do, without words.

When small children want to be picked up, they

normally raise both arms over their head. In Mimi's case, when she wanted to be picked up she only raised her left arm. However, each time, just before picking her up, I gently lifted and stretched her right arm to show her that the signal to be picked up was to raise both arms. It took some time, but gradually she started lifting them both whenever she wanted to be picked up. The right arm didn't reach up as quickly or stretch up as far as the left one but the beginning of a new pattern was there. Besides showing her that the right arm could be used, each time she raised it she was giving the muscles in that arm the stretching they very much needed. It was the same thing with hugging. Mimi's automatic way to hug was with her left arm only, while the right one stayed curled up in its stroke-affected position. But, every time that I hugged her, which was many times throughout the day and every time she sat in my lap and put her arm around my neck, which was also many times a day, I always brought her right arm up and around my neck until she eventually started making the effort to use both arms for this action too.

At one of the early doctor's appointments in a specialized clinic, Mimi was crying and wanted to be picked up. She lifted both arms because even in her distress, it had, by that time, become her reflex to do so. The doctor immediately noticed and commented that it was not common to see a child who has suffered a stroke raise both arms like Mimi had just done. That was my firefly—I knew that Mimi's action was neither accidental nor coincidental. Mimi too had only been using one arm but slowly and surely, gently and lovingly, I had shown her that both arms have a role in being picked up and that both arms are part of giving a hug. It wasn't a change that anyone else had noticed but just like with the piano lessons, I knew what the situation had been at the outset, how much I had been persevering over the past year and what a major accomplishment it was for her. The fact that the doctor noticed the result was incredibly important to me. It was a validation of what my intuition had been telling me—the importance of helping Mimi understand that the "other" arm and hand also had a purpose even though she was far too young for me to explain it to her in words. That one comment was pivotal and encouraged me to continue persevering. It was a particularly bright firefly in my early collection.

Eventually, when Mimi started learning to speak, the flickers of light were easier to see and my collection slowly grew brighter. Even when she could only speak a handful of words, Mimi found creative ways of combining the words that she knew to communicate all kinds of things. Again, I took that as another indication that she was not to be underestimated and that I had every reason to keep persevering. For example, one day we were having lentil soup for lunch. Admittedly, with its brown, murky colour, lentil soup is not necessarily the most delicious-looking of foods. Mimi looked at her soup and then, emphatically, with a look of complete disgust on her face, said, "Mean...dirty...pits!" It was summer and she loved eating cherries, so I guess she figured that the lentils were some kind of smallish cherry pit and since the soup was an ugly brown colour, it was "mean and dirty". Those were about the only negative words that she knew. It was one of her first sentences and I was thrilled to see that she was obviously alert, taking in information from the world around her and creatively applying the words that she was learning to new things.

When Mimi started to speak more fluently, there were even more encouraging signs. Her absolute favourite sentence was "*Mimi do it,*" which she repeated, with emphasis, throughout the day. It didn't matter how complex the task was or that her right hand, at that time, was completely twisted to the side, closed-up and largely unresponsive. Mimi was very clear—she was going to do "it", whatever "it" was, herself. As she got older and had a wider vocabulary, her favourite sentence, on a similar theme, became "I can do it my-*seff*", with a strong emphasis on the "seff". It was abundantly clear that she did indeed have a very strong sense of self, or "seff", as she called it, and it didn't seem right that I should underestimate her because of a little dark spot on a picture somewhere in her file.

When Mimi was two years old, she attended a preschool two mornings a week. Up until then, we had always called her by her given name which is Amelia. She, however, called herself "Mimi" which I had assumed was because she couldn't yet say her name. After one of her first days at preschool, Mimi brought home a painting and on the top of it was written "Mimi". After telling her what a great job she had done, I began explaining that her name was Amelia and that is what she was going to be called at school. She looked at me angrily and said, "Mimi name no *Melia*, Mimi name *Mimi*!!" It was clear what she was telling me. Her name was not "Melia" as we had been calling her, otherwise she too would have been saying that when referring to herself. Her name was Mimi. That is what she had told the parent volunteer at the preschool to write on the top of her painting and that is what we were to call her. And so, that's what we've done. Mimi was only two years old but there was no doubt in my mind that she was thinking clearly and that she wasn't afraid to express "her-seff".

- ◆ -

The reasons that inspired me to keep persevering sometimes came, ironically, packaged in discouraging messages. When Mimi was about six years old, she started scoring very low on tests designed to indicate whether or not she might have learning difficulties, part of which was tested by her ability to do puzzles. After one particular test, I was told that as a result of the way that she had performed, I could expect that

Mimi would not do very well in math as she got older. It was true that Mimi had been doing the puzzles very slowly. She seemed to be putting the pieces down quickly without turning them around to see if they might fit somewhere. It was as if she was not making the link between what she was seeing and what she was supposed to do.

But for me, with all of the flickers of hope that I had already collected by then, there was a possibility that it was not a question of incapacity but rather, a question of strategy and practice. And, strategy is logic, which is looking at things and then doing them one step at a time. So, that same week I bought a number of puzzles and a variety of games that were logic and strategy-based. As I had been told, at first Mimi was very slow at doing these activities. But she, of course, didn't know that she had been assessed as not being particularly good at them and with her "I can do it my-seff" attitude, it wasn't hard to get her to keep trying.

When it came to puzzles, I explained how you can start by finding all of the pieces that have a straight edge. Then, with those pieces, you can put together the outer edges of the puzzle. After that, you can sort the rest of the pieces by colour or pattern. Finally, starting with those piles, you can see if there are any, within each pile, that might fit together. I showed Mimi how you can take one piece at a time and turn it to see if it fits with some of the other pieces. Slowly, Mimi started applying the concepts that I was showing her and she started getting better at both the puzzles and the more complicated games of strategy. The more she played the games and the more I saw that she was learning, the more reasons I had to keep persevering.

Despite Mimi's progress, there was still, however, a fair amount of discouragement. Two years later, Mimi scored very low on another test designed to gauge whether or not she had learning difficulties. She scored in the second percentile—

a very low result indeed. I was told that this time it was certain that the results indicated a problem with her ability to learn, regardless of whatever limitations she had already overcome. Admittedly, I was incredibly discouraged by the result and what I was being told. I was tired from years of always hearing what was not possible. I started asking myself if maybe, this time, I had reached the limit of what I could do to help my daughter. Perhaps, instead of continuing to persevere, a good dose of acceptance on my part was finally in order. That's what I was being told to do, in any case. But, by that time, I had collected so many little flickers of light that it just wasn't in me to simply accept the result without at least persevering in some small way. After all, if I did nothing, then it was very likely that the situation would not improve and if I did something, anything, then there was always a chance for improvement, no matter how small and imperceptible it might be to others.

As a first step, I decided that I would pay much more attention to Mimi's math homework. She had, in fact, started saying that there were things in class that she wasn't understanding. In spending more time reviewing her school work with her, what I found was that Mimi could learn the concepts but she sometimes needed to see a visual representation of the problem. She was helped by having concepts explained to her several times and in several different ways. I asked her to try to tell me, as much as she could, which part of the question she wasn't sure about. Then, I focused on that specific area, eventually tying it back to the overall problem. Whether it was division, fractions, multiplication or any other math problem, my standard line was, "Wait, let me get the chickpeas..." and that's what I used to demonstrate the various concepts. Lentils were too small to manipulate in order to make the various categories of numbers and chocolate chips were too tempting so there was always the risk that the numbers might not add up in the end. No matter how long it took, I tried to stay positive,

I praised her to keep her motivated and I tried to make it fun—as much fun as dried chickpeas can be.

Besides helping Mimi understand her schoolwork, it was important to me to make sure, as much as possible, that she did not feel completely lost as she sat at her desk while the teacher moved forward with the lessons. I wanted to avoid her having that uncomfortable feeling of not knowing what the teacher was talking about, being too afraid to ask for help and knowing that even if she worked up the courage to raise her hand, she might not even be sure how to start the question. Such a situation would definitely serve to erode her sense of "seff" over the longer-term. It wasn't easy and there was definitely some silent frustration and "pati" mixed in with my perseverance but I could see that Mimi did have the capacity to understand and apply various math concepts. What I needed to do was figure out how to explain them to her in a way that worked for her.

Slowly, I could see that Mimi was beginning to feel more comfortable with the math and equally importantly, she was starting to feel more confident in her ability to learn it. At the end of that same school year, I bought a math workbook that covered the concepts that would be taught in the next grade with a view to working with her over the summer. We didn't do math problems every day and we didn't complete the entire workbook but for a number of weeks we sat together for a while and worked through some of the problems. Sometimes we played school and as Mimi started to understand a particular concept we pretended that she was the teacher and she had to explain it to me. Sometimes we sat in the shade under a tree and sometimes we worked through the problems quickly because there was a tasty snack waiting for us afterwards...

That fall, Mimi did not struggle in the same way as she had the previous year. Even if she couldn't remember exactly what my explanation had been over the summer, at least she recognized that it was something that she had already seen and worked on. As a result, she was much less stressed by the teacher's lessons and with that, came the confidence to persevere, with no erosion to her sense of "seff". Not long after that, Mimi was given the exact same test that she had been given the year before—the one on which she had scored in the second percentile. This time, almost exactly one year later, Mimi scored in the *ninety*-second percentile. I knew that the result was no accident. Since the last time she had taken the test, Mimi had worked through a lot of reasoning, logic and thinking activities.

It is possible, that because of the stroke, Mimi does have more difficultly learning certain things. Nevertheless, I don't think it means that limitations should immediately be put on her and that she should be underestimated. From my perspective, given patience, time, encouragement and a whole lot of dried chickpeas, there is always reason to be hopeful—there is reason to persevere.

– ◆ –

Now, with the progress that Mimi has made I no longer need to constantly be on the lookout for little flickers of hope. They are all around me and sometimes they are so bright that they surprise me. For example, when the girls were small, my parents and I started taking them ice skating. Where we live, the winters are long and you don't necessarily have to be a figure skating champion but you need to at least be able to get around on the ice. It's hard to learn to skate at the best of times and in Mimi's case, there was the added challenge of the weakness of her right ankle, her limited ability to balance on her right leg, and the muscle tightness in her right foot. Even so, we kept on persevering. Mimi wore a helmet, of course, and she had snow pants on to soften the impact when she fell.

I held her up as securely as I could so she was as safe as any-one can be standing on a slippery frozen surface with sharp blades strapped to their feet. It was slow and it took several winters before she could even just keep her balance enough to stand on the ice but eventually, she learned to do it. Then, very slowly, she learned to move around on the ice. I'm not sure that I would really call it skating. Initially, it was more of a lopsided two-blades-on-the-ice-at-the-same-time-shuffle but she could get around. That was good enough. It was a major success and another flicker of hope.

When Mimi was eight years old, she changed schools and at the new school, the physical education program included skating lessons. Once a week, I made sure that she had her skates, a helmet and a pair of mittens with her when I dropped her off at school. I wondered how she would do without me helping her and what the teacher would make of her lopsided shuffle. But by then she was at an age where I had to start letting go. I had to trust that she could manage at school and trust that her teachers would help her as needed. Towards the end of the school year, Mimi started talking about the year-end skating show that her class was working on. The details were vague but she said that I needed to get her a pair of beige tights, and the rest of the costume would be taken care of by the school. So, on the day of the skating show I dropped Mimi off at school with her skates and requisite beige tights and after school, Charlotte and I went to the arena. I had no idea what to expect as the tights were not much of a clue for what was to come.

When we got to the arena, the bleachers were packed full of happy families waiting with anticipation to see the show. The rink had been turned into a veritable ice skating palace with a stage, curtains, lighting and decorations. Already, just seeing the rink transformed, I realized that the event was going to be much more elaborate than I had expected. Then, the lights dimmed and the first group of students came out onto the ice. It was the grade after Mimi's, so all of the kids were one year older than her. I watched as they came out onto the ice, one at a time. First, they formed a single line. Then, they split into two lines, and then three lines, and then four lines and then finally, there were five lines of children all skating precisely in time to the music. Then, those five lines joined in the middle to form what looked like the spokes of a wheel. And finally, to my amazement, those five lines of children started skating in a circular motion for a fantastic on-ice Rockettes-style effect!

It was very impressive. I had assumed that the school's skating lessons would simply be covering the basics of getting around on the ice—I wasn't expecting elaborately choreographed numbers. As I watched those older kids, I immediately felt a lump in my chest as I thought about Mimi. My mind was racing, wondering how I would find a skating rink that stayed open over the summer in order to make sure that by the following year, Mimi would have some hope of keeping up with what was expected in the next grade. I couldn't picture how, with her wobbly, shuffling skating self, she would ever be able to participate in those fancy ice-skating formations.

At last, it was time for Mimi's class to skate. The lights dimmed, the music started and the kids began coming out onto the ice. Along with the bland beige tights that I had sent along, the teachers had added a black skirt and a sparkly striped shirt. One by one, the kids came out from behind the curtains, skated forward and formed a single line. Then, they split into two lines, and then three lines, and then four lines and finally, there were five lines of children all skating precisely in time to the music. Then, those five lines joined in the middle to make what looked like the spokes of a wheel, and then...those five lines of children started skating in a circular motion for a fantastic on-ice Rockettes-style effect! I could not believe what I was seeing—in the middle of those fancy on-ice manoeuvres, smiling happily and confidently, was my Mimi!! Charlotte and I were on the edge of our seats, watching Mimi with complete amazement. We were hugging each other with great big tears of pride and happiness in our eyes. When the music stopped, there was no one in that arena clapping louder than the two of us.

When I saw Mimi after the show I hugged her tightly and said, "That was fantastic, my sweetie! I didn't know you could do all of that!" Mimi looked at me rather surprised and said matter-of-factly, "I knew, Mama." That's exactly right, she knew. The over-protective mother in me had temporarily over-shadowed my inner collection of firefly light. But Mimi isn't relying on me to provide her with inspiration and reasons to persevere. She knows who she is and she knows that she is capable of doing whatever it is that she wants to do—little dark spot or no little dark spot. Mimi clearly already has, within her-seff, a glowing source of strength that motivates her to persevere.

With that realization, I quietly added a particularly bright firefly to my own collection.

12

Landing Safely Someplace New

When I had imagined, so long ago, what it would be like to work as a flight attendant, I had pictured it as incredibly glamorous and exciting all of the time. And, in the beginning, having just graduated from the illustrious flight attendant training program, it was with great excitement that I looked over my schedule of flights. I couldn't wait to see where I would be going. London? Paris? Helsinki, maybe? Eventually though, it became a job like any other. I showed up for work, did whatever I had to do and when I had finished, I went home. This was particularly true for what they called "turnarounds". These were flights that travelled south with a planeload of pale, tired-looking passengers and then turned around and came right back the same day with a different load of tanned, boisterous, mostly hungover passengers. On those flights, it didn't really matter where we were going because we normally didn't step off the aircraft until we were back home again, twelve hours later.

At the end of the first half of one such turnaround, the plane was coming in for a landing and I was sitting at the front of the aircraft in a jump seat (the fold-down seat for flight attendants). Beside me, looking equally official and "flight ready" in his blue polyester suit and maroon tie, was the in-flight service manager. Along with making sure that everything went smoothly on the flight, it was his job to make all of the announcements. As the plane landed and started slowing down, he picked up the microphone to announce our arrival. He pressed the lever on the side of the microphone and cheerfully said, "Good morning ladies and gentlemen and welcome to..." He paused, then started again, "Welcome to..." He released the lever, looked at me and said, "Where are we?!" I looked back at him and said, "We're, we're...uhh..." I was frantically trying to remember where we were but finally had to admit that I had absolutely no idea.

We burst out laughing at the realization that neither one of us knew where the plane had just touched down. It could have been anywhere. With a great deal of embarrassment, we asked one of the passengers sitting in the front row immediately across from us and she answered, "San José...I hope." So, red-faced and laughing, he started his announcements again, followed by the usual warnings to remain seated until the aircraft has come to a complete stop and to be careful when opening the overhead bins. I looked out the window and thought to myself, *That's funny...this place looks kind of misty and jungle-like for California.* As it turns out, it was kind of misty and jungle-like. It was much later that I realized that we had been in San José, Costa Rica, not California.

The feeling that I had that day, not quite sure where I was but knowing that I had at least landed safely someplace after travelling a great distance, was something that I would feel again later in my life. I had been travelling along on my life's journey, following the flight plan that I had set for myself towards a happy and fulfilling family life. I can't pinpoint exactly when the acute turbulence started. I guess it was somewhere between Mimi's diagnosis and the unravelling of my marriage, but at some point my life started spiralling out of control. I had no idea which way was up and which way was down. I had no idea where I was headed or how I was going to take care of my two young passengers along the way.

At that time, all I could do was look at each day as a 24-hour capsule. In each capsule, there were all of the "macro" challenges that had to be dealt with, like securing a livelihood and dealing with the end of my marriage. And, there was the multitude of daily "micro" challenges, like getting Mimi to her appointments on time and making sure that Charlotte also got all the care and attention that she needed. Obviously, it was the "macro" challenges that caused the most turbulence in my life but no matter what, within every 24-hour capsule, I did whatever I could on all fronts.

Eventually, one by one, I managed to resolve the "macro" issues. There was no celebration when I finally signed the papers for a full-time job but it was a major accomplishment for me nonetheless and it removed a major source of turbulence in my life. Although it took longer than I thought it would, eventually papers were also signed to formalise the end of my marriage. I felt sad that it had turned out the way it had but at the same time, it was a relief that it was over. That source of turbulence was now also behind me.

Slowly, as I resolved the bigger problems, as I started to see that Mimi could hold her own in the "mainstream", as the girls began to thrive in our new life and as the Goldberg Variations helped me to breathe without feeling like I was gasping for some unseen oxygen mask, the 24-hour capsules were increasingly filled with the smaller challenges of everyday life. With time, it really did seem as if I had safely landed someplace new. I wasn't really sure where that someplace was or if it would end up being my final destination. But, it felt like my feet were, at last, firmly on the ground even if it was still a bit shaky now and again.

Unlike my flight attendant days, however, there was no cheerful announcement confirming that I had arrived at this new destination and, since I was travelling alone, there was no one sitting across from me to ask. It had all come about so very slowly. Part of it, was that with the resolution of each issue, came another series of related issues. For example, along with the realization that my man-on-the-moon-sized goal of "mainstream by grade one" was going to become a reality, came the realization that there were now dozens of new challenges to be sorted out. For starters, in the mainstream, how was Mimi going to put her knapsack on by herself? At that time, she wasn't quite four years old and the use of her right arm was much more limited than it is now.

The answer, thanks to the advice of an occupational therapist, was that Mimi could use her left arm to put one strap over her right shoulder and then put her left arm through the other strap to get the knapsack on her back. It worked perfectly, she just had to do it exactly the same way every time, using her left arm to compensate for the right one. All in all, it didn't matter if Mimi put her knapsack on differently from the other children. I doubt that any of them even noticed. But, by anticipating what she would need to do and giving her a strategy for doing it herself, I avoided a situation in which she would feel different or incapable. Still, it had been a "micro" issue for which a solution had had to be found over a number of 24-hour capsules.

Along with the knapsack, there was the challenge of how Mimi would open her snack and lunch containers. We tried different shapes and sizes to see which ones she might be able to open herself and then practiced to make sure that when snack time came around, she would be able to manage on her own. Again, Mimi's way was a little different. She had to hold the container in the crook of her right arm and then use her left hand to take the lid off. But, with some practice, she could do it. I had tears in my eyes the day that I asked Mimi's teacher how she was doing in class and she told me that Mimi was actually the one helping some of the other kids with their containers. I was so proud of her—another little firefly of hope inspiring me to keep persevering.

Zippers were a much bigger challenge. In the first couple of years, it didn't matter all that much because hardly any of the kids could do up their own jackets. As they got older, however, and became more independent, I had to find a solution for Mimi. After all, I couldn't expect her to maintain a strong sense of self if she was the only one asking the teacher for help to get dressed, as the others looked on. That would have been the perfect recipe for teasing in the playground and erosion of sense of self in the school environment. The problem was, that although Mimi could easily manipulate the zipper pull with her left hand, she was completely unable to use her right hand to hold back the flaps of fabric that covered the zipper and then, hold the two sides together to zip up.

In my first attempt to deal with this challenge, I used two large metal clips to hold back the flaps of fabric. My reasoning was that in addition to enabling Mimi to concentrate on simply threading the two sides of the zipper together, the clips would give her something bigger to hold onto. Unfortunately, no matter how I placed them, the clips popped off as soon as Mimi tried to grab onto them. My next idea was to take Mimi's jacket to a seamstress and have her sew the flaps of fabric back, away from the zipper. The result of this variation was much more promising. Mimi really struggled—sometimes the right hand was cooperative and sometimes it wasn't but she kept on trying. That summer, I had Mimi practise with that same zipper many, many times and by the time the cold weather came the following school year, Mimi was ready. It took her longer to get her jacket on but she could do it by herself. It was a tiny triumph over a "micro" challenge, one year in the making.

Although she had mastered zipping up her winter jacket, many more challenges remained. Mimi still had trouble with zippers on items of clothing that were less bulky, like sweaters and sweatshirts, for example. Buttons were also a major challenge. It seemed a lot less likely that she would ever be able to button up a shirt than it had been likely that Neil Armstrong's boots would ever get moon dust on them. But, each day, each challenge and each eventual tiny triumph led us to the next day and the next set of challenges and eventually, we found ourselves doing math with the dried chickpeas. Along the way, what I found particularly inspiring was that as soon as Mimi's ability to use her right hand increased even slightly, she applied that new capacity to all kinds of other activities.

For example, when she was finally able to keep her right hand open for a few seconds, although it was still twisted to the side and largely unresponsive, Mimi figured out a way to tie her hair with an elastic. To expand on that skill, since no girl wants a messy-looking ponytail, we played a game called "beauty parlour". Mimi was the hairdresser and I was the client, always on my way to a fancy party and in need of an appropriately fancy hairdo. Given that the underlying theme of this game was to get Mimi to improve the use of her right hand and the extent to which she used both hands together, I would encourage her to tie up as much hair as she could. I bought a big package of multicoloured elastics and each tuft of hair that she tied up with those elastics was a tiny triumph.

Slowly, Mimi got better and better at it, which eventually translated into her being able to make her own tidy ponytails. As far as my own appearance during the game, however, I would say that there was much more parlour than beauty, judging from the multicoloured hedgehog that was normally looking back at me in the mirror. And that's how it went. The 24-hour capsules blended together into weeks, months and years, and as time went by, I realized that I was in some new place. Instead of the turbulence from before, my 24-hour capsules were mostly filled with normal day-to-day activities.

In this new place, far away from the devastating appointment with that first specialist, Mimi and I have had the opportunity to consult with many wonderful doctors, specialists, occupational, speech and physiotherapists, not to mention the ingenious people who specialize in creating the orthopedic hand and foot braces that have been so helpful to us. Collectively, these professionals continue to provide us with the guidance we need to make sure that Mimi will eventually have the capacity to do, as much as possible, all of the things that will one day be the foundation of her own day-to-day activities. In this new place, there are still problems to be solved and rehabilitation challenges to be overcome. But overall, instead of chaos, now there is routine, instead of fear, there is optimism, instead of a sense of panic, there is stability and instead of a lot of sadness, now there is much more fun and laughter.

I still love listening to the Goldberg Variations but now, it is no longer for the same reasons. Over the years, the "music nights" have been replaced by other more light-hearted activities. In the winter it can be "movie night" or "new recipe night" and in the summer, Friday nights are often "picnic nights". As we sit together on the grass, talking, laughing, eating and looking up at the clouds to see what funny shapes we can find, I always think of what Friday nights used to mean—how exhausted I used to be, how scared I used to feel and how close to the edge I actually was. Thankfully, that place seems very far behind me now.

These days, although Mimi still has occupational and physiotherapy appointments, there are very few medical appointments for us to go to. Now, it's mostly school, music, skating and soccer events that I attend, for the most part, alone. That is, alone in the sense that there is no other adult with me.

It's OK though. If it's Charlotte's event, then Mimi sits beside me and if it's Mimi's event, then Charlotte sits beside me. We take great pride in each other. We are a family. I love them and they love me. It is truly a happy and fulfilling family life, just as I have always wanted.

My eyes still fill up as I sit quietly watching the girls at their various events but unlike the burning tears that used to leak out when I sat alone in the hospital waiting rooms, now they are tears of pride, relief and joy. When I start to feel overwhelmed by emotion, I remind myself how far we've come, what a strong sense of family I have fostered between the three of us and the stability that I have worked so hard to secure for us.

Then, I remind myself to breathe normally and trust that everything is going to be fine. And in this new place, it is.

13

The Beauty of Mosaics

When Charlotte was ten years old, she participated in an after school mosaic workshop. I have never worked with tiles but I have seen my father successfully tackle a lot of renovation projects so I know how much precision and skill is required to get everything to look just right. It sounded like a rather advanced undertaking for a child of her age but I looked forward to seeing the final result. Each week, Charlotte came home and excitedly told me how her project was coming along and when she finally brought it home, it was magnificent.

The instructions had been to take a small mirror and glue it onto a wooden base and then, take broken bits of tile to create a pattern all around the mirror. Charlotte said that most of the children had put the mirror in the middle and after that, created a symmetrical pattern all around to fill in the rest of the space. Charlotte, however, had a vision. Rather than just randomly creating a pattern, she had painstakingly created a garden scene. Using yellow and black bits of tile, she had created an adorable little bumble bee. From red and black bits of tile, she had created a beautiful little lady bug, and from pink and orange bits of tile, she had made a delicate butterfly. Along one side was a linear pattern of blue flowers with shiny orange centres and tying the entire scene together was a background of sweeping two-toned blades of grass. Up close, you could see how she had taken dozens and dozens of little pieces of broken tile of all shapes, colours and sizes and meticulously pieced them together. But from a distance, you could see how all of the groupings of little pieces blended together perfectly to create individual elements and, at the same time, a spectacularly harmonious picture.

In many ways, I see my own life much as I do Charlotte's mosaic. Just like Charlotte had a vision of what she wanted to create and then, with patience and perseverance, made it a reality, I had a vision of how I wanted my life to be. Instead of a mirror in the middle of my life's mosaic, what I wanted in the centre was a happy and fulfilling family life. Then, all around that centre would be everything else that is part of life—unavoidable realities and responsibilities but also, all of the things that add to life's beauty. A significant part of that beauty has come from appreciating what is positive, rather than dwelling on what is not.

In particular, it is true that I have faced the challenges of Mimi's rehabilitation alone and that I have found myself navigating through many difficult situations on my own. It is also true that I spent many years feeling lonely and isolated, only to ultimately find myself raising my daughters alone and isolated. In and around this reality, however, there has also been support and kindness—there have been all kinds of beautiful little pieces of "tile" that have fit in to help the girls and me. Sometimes, like the pieces of tile in Charlotte's project, the pieces in the mosaic of my life have also been sharp and jagged. On their own, these jagged pieces, like feeling that my wellbeing and that of our daughters was not important to my ex-husband, or the emotional isolation that I felt in my childhood, have caused me much pain over the years. However, in the context of my mosaic, with the wellbeing of my daughters as the primary theme, or the grout that holds everything together, even these sharp pieces have helped create the overall beauty. For example, although my ex-husband has not been involved in our daughters' everyday lives, on the days that he visits, he provides the love and support that he can. And, he has even been a part of helping Mimi with certain key accomplishments, like her ability to ride a bicycle.

Teaching Mimi to ride a bike was a multi-year, multi-person project. First, my father took her out on her tricycle for several summers in a row to get her used to gripping the handlebars, steering and pedalling. It was tricky and mostly, he just pushed her along, but eventually she learned to pedal and you could see how delighted she was to feel the sense of freedom that comes from racing around on a tricycle. After that, she graduated to a scooter. I figured that with a scooter, she would learn to keep her balance but it wouldn't be quite as difficult or dangerous as a bicycle. At first, I held the handlebars for her and walked slowly beside her. It was tedious, but two summers later I could barely keep up with her as I ran alongside.

Having mastered the scooter, I thought that she might be ready to try riding a bicycle. But by that time, she was too heavy for me to be able to hold the bike steady while she sat on it. So, each time that her father came to visit, he helped her in the parking lot behind our building, armed with the advice that the occupational and physiotherapists had given me. From the balcony, I could see him gently coaching her and holding the bike upright by the back of the seat, while Mimi did her best to keep her balance and steer.

On the day that she actually managed to ride her bike on her own, there was much rejoicing. It was Father's Day. Mimi was triumphantly circling the parking lot on her first solo ride, with her father running along beside her, arms outstretched, ready to catch her in case she fell. Charlotte was riding her bike in big celebratory circles around the main event, smiling happily at Mimi while I stood on the balcony clapping and cheering excitedly. It wasn't exactly the circumstances that I had pictured as a happy and fulfilling family life so long ago but it was beautiful nonetheless and I appreciated everything that that moment represented. On their own, perhaps my dad taking Mimi out on her tricycle and me taking her out on her scooter, might have been individual, isolated pieces in my mosaic. But put together with the efforts of her father, all of those little pieces ultimately fit together, much like the broken bits of tile in Charlotte's mosaic, to create one specific element. In this case, Mimi's ability to ride a bike.

The same is true for some of Mimi's other accomplishments. For the last few summers, with the guidance of Mimi's occupational therapist, we have set specific goals. Without school and homework, the long summer days are perfect for fitting in rehabilitation activities. One year, it was developing Mimi's ability to cut food with a knife and fork. To most people, this may seem like a basic task but to someone who has suffered a stroke, it is a major challenge requiring an enormous investment of time and effort. As the school year ends, I start the process and begin composing "variations" on whatever it is that we've decided to work towards. Then, later in the summer, when the girls spend time with my parents, my mother fills in.

In these cases, it is all of our efforts together, no matter how jagged our inter-relationships might feel outside of the context of the girls' well-being, that fit together to create a single beautiful element in the overall picture.

- ◆ -

They say that time heals all wounds but I'm not sure I really believe that. I do believe, however, that with each passing day, as we add new pieces of tile to our mosaics and focus our efforts on particular areas, the jagged edges of a painful experience soften and overall, it starts to hurt less. As our mosaics evolve and as we look at things with the distance that comes with time, the memories blur and eventually there can be a sense of healing. At least that's how it feels for me.

The combined effect of finding out that my daughter had suffered a stroke, coping with the emotions that the diagnosis brought on, struggling to help her in a context that was suffocatingly discouraging and dealing with a series of other unexpected challenges in that same period of time, was a major wound in my life. But now, almost ten years later, enough wonderful things have happened in-between that the memories of what was so painful are definitely fading. In their place, is the optimism that comes from seeing my daughters thriving, the sense of strength that comes from seeing the results of my perseverance, particularly with respect to overcoming the effects of Mimi's stroke, and the freedom to dream about the future that comes from being further and further away from what was so painful. As it turns out, the seemingly unrelated pieces of my past have all fit together to help create the happy and fulfilling family life that I have always wanted—the mirror in the centre of my own life's mosaic—along with all of the extraordinary beauty that is all around it.

The long hours I spent sitting in my room reading Nancy Drew books as a child and the endless trips to the local library helped open my mind to other ways of thinking, which eventually guided my choices later in life. My experience working in the government, where you put your emotions aside and think analytically, helped me to know exactly how to go about defining clear goals, even under pressure and then set myself up to achieve them. Working as a flight attendant, which seemed like a rather frivolous summer job at the time, ended up providing me with reference points for effectively getting myself out of an excruciatingly turbulent period in my life. My love of music and playing the piano served as an important framework for figuring out how to approach, and then sustain, Mimi's rehabilitation activities. All of these pieces of tile are there, somewhere in my mosaic, along with the countless contributions of friendship and support from so many others, which collectively expand the sense of family beyond the mirror in the middle.

Even the jagged and painful pieces of the past have ultimately contributed something positive. The emotional isolation that I felt as a child ended up giving me the ability to get through a period of overlapping crises alone, even though it was at that very time that I most needed to be comforted. The episode at the music school, in which the director unwittingly uncorked all of my inner anguish by discriminating against Mimi, ended up leading to a period of healing along with a resolve to do something constructive with my experience. It's strange to say, but even the specialist in his lab coat, whose negativity and closed-mindedness was so painful to me, is part of the overall beauty of my mosaic. In the early years, the anger that I felt as a result of his discouraging attitude fuelled a relentless determination to prove him wrong which, in part, brought many of Mimi's earliest triumphs.

On the other hand, I would have been just as determined and effective, probably even more so, if I had had a positive reference point. Instead of being driven by outrage and fear, I could have been motivated by hope, which would have been much more constructive and infinitely less painful. Perhaps my own story can be just that kind of a reference point in the mosaic of someone else's life. That is my sincere hope.

The specialist was right about one thing though. In Mimi's mosaic there will always be a little dark spot. It is permanent, just like he said—a wound that time will never heal. But, all around, there are countless beautiful pieces of tile of all shapes and colours. I am certain that as Mimi grows older and builds on the mosaic of her own life, the little dark spot, no matter how permanent, will be less and less noticeable.

In fact, even now, sometimes when I take a step back and see how much beauty, love and success there already is, I can hardly see it at all.